Women's Stories,
Women's Voices

WOMEN'S STORIES, WOMEN'S VOICES
Victoria Villaseñor and Nicci Robinson, Editors
Global Words Press
Copyright retained by individual authors
Cover Design by OceanFlame Photography
Internal Artwork by A.J. Meakin
Collection copyright © 2016 Global Words Press
Imprint Digital, UK
Cataloging information
ISBN: 978-1-911227-08-3

WOMEN'S STORIES, WOMEN'S VOICES

2016
GLOBAL WORDS PRESS
NOTTINGHAM, UK

What's Your Story?

FOREWORD

O n behalf of NIDAS (Nottinghamshire Independent Domestic Abuse Services) it's my great honour to be asked to introduce this book. Some of these short stories have been carefully scripted by survivors of domestic abuse who have, along with the thoughtful and supportive guidance of Global Wordsmiths, been able to capture the personal and intimate journeys of the trauma they have experienced and situations overcome. The objective of capturing these real life events are to share, inspire, teach and inform others in like situations, past and present, that no one has to suffer in silence and that support is available. In addition, these stories are a celebration of the places survivors have travelled from, to allow their voices to be heard.

At the time Global Wordsmiths approached our project to become involved, we were re-positioning ourselves in the community of Mansfield and Ashfield as a destination provider for children and young people. As an independent domestic abuse support agency established in 1986 we listened to what our community told us and re-launched our service, adopting a new whole-family approach, putting children and young people are the heart of what we do, and moving away from providing support from women and children individually.

As an innovative agency, we strive to focus on ways to work together with other agencies, to raise awareness, and be part of driving change in attitudes. I have the highest praise and recognition for the courage and strength of the women who have written for this anthology, and in particular a few of the young people from our NIDAS community who volunteered to share their experiences. I further extend sincere thanks to our dedicated team who work tirelessly to continue to provide tailored support at our services, and finally to the Global Wordsmiths team who have succeeded in bringing this book to life.

Lisa Haydon-Bennett
Director of Service, NIDAS

PREFACE

Women are still second-class citizens. We are still seen as the *weaker* sex. Despite many successes in empowering women, many issues still exist in all areas of life, ranging from the cultural and political to the economic. Women often work more than men yet are paid less; gender discrimination affects girls and women throughout their lifetime; and women and girls are often the ones that suffer the most poverty. Women suffer. Girls suffer. The Government have instigated funds to tackle "Violence against Women and Girls," and when your read some of the following stories, you'll be in no doubt as to why such funding is an absolute necessity.

This book began as a project with NIDAS. We delivered weekly workshops which encouraged a group of survivors to share their difficult and distressing experiences. It became so difficult for some that we ended up with just three extremely brave under-sixteens who saw them through to the end, and a worker whose past experience enhances her empathy to work with domestic violence survivors.

In an effort to make sure these women's stories were told, an open submissions call ensued, and we were inundated with girls and women from all over the world who had a desire to be heard. Their voices, in these stories, are a poignant, fascinating walk through various cultures and experiences. Some are funny, some are sad, some are full of wonder, and some are very difficult to read. We are incredibly proud to send this book out into the world where women's stories and women's voices are so desperately needed.

~Nicci Robinson, Ed.

CONTENTS

MIDWIFERY OF THE FUTURE
By Nina Dauban

If you have fallen in love with your part as an Agent of
Change
If you courted that destiny to make yourself fit to Serve
If you are married to the Mission without compromise
If you have consummated that communion with others of
kind
Then you will be pregnant with the Future and in need of
Midwifery

If your willing readiness is wobbled by the occasional
glimpse of
"Life will never be the same again"
If your excitement is thrilled to witness the new theatres of
Humanity
If the reality looms large that it's going to be on Its terms not
yours
Know that birth is visiting you, nudging you into Alignment

As some of the pixels of Evolution's canvas become clear
A new oxygen liberates the Creativity of all who breath deep
Know you are lining the womb with the guarantee of your
standards
And decorating the nursery with every brush stroke of
devotion

When the stretch comes and you reach to meet its requirement
The Midwife provides you with the assurance That you were born for This
She knows that the fruits of your labour will bring blessings beyond imagination
Her confidence and gentle authority make you feel safe and all is well

In the final hours as the enormity of Evolution emerges from its plasma
The Midwife covers you in the presence of Connected Stillness
The Lone state is Never to be felt again as you are born into your Creation destiny
A homecoming and Unification with All Life and LOVE itself.

BED RIDDANCE
By Emily Richards

Hello, my name is Lily Thompson and I am "Bed Ridden." Have you ever thought about that phrase? "Bed Ridden?" What does it mean? I'm riding the bed? The world's got rid of me at last: sent me to bed? I've heard the phrase all my life. Bet you have too, but I've never really sat down and thought about it for long, realised how silly it is. I've plenty of time to sit down now. Maybe there's another meaning of "ridden" that I don't know. Probably. There's lots of meanings I don't know: I left school at fourteen. Didn't want to wear glasses to read the board, see. *Boys don't make passes at girls who wear glasses.* Worked though, didn't it? Married before my twentieth birthday. For what that's worth now. Now that I'm bedridden, no husband left to visit. And the NHS would have given me a bed anyway, whether Derek had been able to afford it or not.

My daughter Elaine was an English teacher, before she retired. She'll know what bed ridden means. Or my granddaughter: she's an English teacher, too. Makes me wonder if being stupid isn't in my bones after all, as me mother was fond of saying. I did a test for dementia once with one of the carers. My score came up as "mild something impairment." Can't remember the middle word. Typical. Elaine told them about me leaving school at fourteen, and they noted it down, said it was a handicap,

3

gave me an extra point. Didn't matter, I was still mildly
impaired. Not impaired enough for a diagnosis, too impaired
to rule it out. None the wiser then on the stupidity front.
I said to them—what's the point in all of this, anyway? To
embarrass me? Isn't Parkinson's, a missing breast, and a
dead husband handicap enough? The only handicap Derek
had was a ten in golf. That bloody man breezed through life.
I'll always look after you, Lily love, he told me. *Stick with me,
duck, I were born lucky.* Well, where are you now, eh, my
lucky duck?

Bed ridden. Chair ridden. Same blummin' difference. I've
been ridden one way or another for years, since Parkinson's
lost me my licence. Well, the two crashes lost me my
licence, but it was Parkinson's fault. I've been doddering
on me zimmer from bed to armchair for three years. Carers
to make breakfast, carers to make tea, carers to wash me
blummin' privates. One cup of tea I wanted to make myself,
tripped over me own feet. That's what's landed me here.
But the bloody joke of it is that now that I've got a fractured
leg, now that I'm bed-ridden, I'm on my feet more than
ever. Blummin' physiotherapy. Blummin' nurse, barely out
of nappies, telling me to think positive, think myself well. I
lived through the war, duck! Ration books! I tell her all this,
tell her to shove her positive mental attitude. She walks off,
mutters "What a sweet old lady." She says it so as I'll hear, so
I let her hear what I've got to say too. I shout it. "If you want
sweet old ladies, go to a W.I. meeting, duck, not a hospital
ward! Old age is serious business, you cheeky cow!" Sweet
old lady indeed. I was never a sweet young lady, why should
I start being sweet now? I'm a human being, not a Werther's
Original! What was that poem Elaine was always going on
about for her O Levels? Rage against the dying of the light!
No one told Dylan Thomas to keep his bloody chin up.

The "think positive" nurse comes back. Gives me some pills "for the pain, *sweetheart*."

"Thanks, *love*." Even under all these wrinkles, even with the blue of my eyes dimmed to grey, my evil eye's better than hers. Still got it, old girl, Derek would say.

I only realise it's Codeine once it's too late. They've been warned not to give it to me. On my little wall chart it says: "Lily, milk no sugar, no opiates (hallucinations)." Too late. She'll get away with it. Overworked NHS. Ah well. How much worse can it be? What was that advice mother gave me about my wedding night? Lie back and think of England? Poor mother. Who knows what she'd have made of the sixties. My wedding night was a blummin' riot. Wouldn't mind being that kind of bed ridden again.

Anyway, I don't think of England. Not this time. In fact, I think of Kilimanjaro. That's in Africa! My grandson went on a trip with his university a few weeks ago—he says he doesn't mind doing it again if I fancy it, he wants to show me the view. Well, we manage the climb in less than half an hour, and that's with the dog in tow. Sammy reckons that's a world record, but I shrug it off. I was always a fast walker when I was young. I treat him to some fruit trifle in the cafe at the peak. He has to leave for a cricket match, so I ask him to drop me off at the theatre on the way. Barbara and I tour London together. She looks amazing—best she's looked since we were at school—her blonde hair in a bob, polka dot dress like she's Marilyn. "You don't look bad for eighty-six, Barb." I laugh, and she says, "We're only young once, Lil, you're looking pretty grand yourself." And then she's hoisting me up on to the stage. The actors don't seem to mind, they're clapping.

"Really, you don't think this is too much?" I'm pointing down at my bush, which is as blonde as Barbara's bob.

"Too much?" She laughs. "Do you see anyone complaining? If you've got it, Lil, flaunt it!"

So I do, firing rainbow lasers from my nipples which I don't remember getting pierced, but I tell you what, it looks blummin' good. I should never have kicked up such a fuss when Elaine got her ears pierced. I should never have kicked up any fusses. I should've spent more time tap dancing naked under the spotlight. I will from now on.

I'll wipe the "no" off my little board when I get back to the hospital. And the bit about hallucinations. I'll add an exclamation mark, add three, I reckon I can get out of bed for that. "Lily! Milk no sugar! Opiates!" My granddaughter'll complain, no doubt.

"Come on, Nana," she'll say in her concerned teacher voice. Bless her, she means well. She'll say, "We want you to walk again."

And I'll say, "Listen ducky, I don't need to walk. Why walk when you can fly?'

The Front Door
By Jan Gayle

I hadn't been home from work long when I heard the ding-dong of our doorbell. I wasn't surprised, but I jumped. I knew who it was—my teenage son. I didn't want to do this. He left home over a month ago, and it had been quiet and stress-free the whole time he was gone.

I felt an uneasy sensation in my stomach and pressure in my chest. I recognised it immediately as that sick feeling I experienced lately whenever I had to talk to him. In less than five months he transformed into a different person—one I didn't like very much. He rang the doorbell because my wife and I changed the locks on the door a week ago when we finally reached our limit. It involved the toxic combination of drugs, two girlfriends, a hatchet, and a baseball bat.

My hand was shaking when I walked to the door and reached for the knob. I wasn't scared, just filled with anxiety. The situation we were in was volatile, and there was really no way of knowing where this would go. I didn't want him back, but I didn't want him to go either.

He greeted me coolly and for just a second our eyes met, and I saw the boy he used to be. Then he pushed past me like he thought he still lived there. As the strong pungent smell of sweat and the noxious scent of his e-cigarettes—a sickly sweet tropical concoction—hit my senses, I withdrew from him. He strutted through the room with his grubby backpack hanging off one shoulder and his skateboard in his hand. I believe he thought he was the coolest thing going despite the stink and the filth, or maybe because of it. His always-present baggy black pants and black T-shirt were stained with grey splotches of unknown origin. If I had to guess I'd say food; the boy couldn't eat without getting whatever it was all over him, but it was really just a guess. Since I didn't even know who he was anymore, how could I know what crap was on his shirt?

I followed him to the kitchen where his mother was sitting, but he kept on going right past her toward his old bedroom.

"Where are you going?" I called to his back.

"Put my stuff down," he yelled back with the "I-know-everything" attitude of a teenager.

"You can set it in here." I said it sternly enough to make my point.

He returned still holding everything and just stood in the hallway staring at me.

"You wanted to talk to us?" I asked and slid onto the barstool next to our high-top dining room table.

"Ahhh, yeah." He dropped his stuff on the floor. I cringed as the skateboard smacked down on the ceramic tile. Settling onto a stool at the kitchen island, he seemed to be searching for words. He picked up a click-top pen that had been lying on the counter and immediately began punching the top repeatedly in a one, two-one, two, three pattern.

No one spoke. My wife and I generally had trouble keeping our mouths shut when he came to talk to us. It always ended up with us doing most of the talking, trying to help him figure out what to say or trying to get him to say what we wanted him to. The silence was beginning to be painful; it felt like everything slowed down to half speed, but

I fought the urge to speak. I wanted to hear what he had to say. I was all talked out.

"Uhh...I wanted to ask you if I could get...uhh...some...you know...money."

I guess I wasn't surprised, but I think I was expecting some kind of apology for his poor behaviour or some explanation about why he needed money, since we knew he had just blown nearly a thousand dollars in less than two weeks—at smoke shops, probably. But no, there was no apology or explanation.

"Why do you need money?" I played dumb. I knew what he wanted the money for. Or at least, I thought I did. But I was also trying to get him to talk, explain, think...something.

"To get an apartment."

"No. I won't lend you money." I didn't say any more. I just wanted this to be the end of it and for him to leave. We had been putting up with it since the first of the year—months and months of stress and worry as we watched him get deeper and deeper into trouble. I knew it wouldn't be the end of the conversation, but I also knew if I started talking it would last longer and get tenser with each word. And frankly, that scared me. For several months he'd been angry all the time, yelling and cursing at us for even the smallest request. He quit his class at the community college three weeks before the class ended. He was smoking cigarettes and doing drugs. I hoped it was only pot, but I wasn't sure. Even though he was only eighteen, he'd found a regular source of booze, and he stayed out most nights with a girl, drinking and smoking weed. The gauges in his ears were growing larger, and he refused to do anything to help around the house. My son had changed.

I don't really know what he expected us to say, but he looked up from the clicking pen with big eyes and leaned back on the stool, appalled.

"I can't get a place then, and I don't have anywhere to live." His deep baritone voice actually went up an octave or two, and the attitude was back.

I held back the angry words I wanted to spew at him. I desperately wanted to point out the countless actions he demonstrated over the last six months that led to this situation. Truthfully, it was pain and sadness over the loss of my sweet, innocent boy. But again I managed to restrain myself. I glanced over at Janet, and she just stared at him. I knew she was using every muscle in her body to keep from exploding with disappointment in her oldest child.

"I can't give you money, but I will give you an alternative to living on the street." Again, I waited. He had to make a decision.

"What?" He looked up from his busy hands again, all the while bouncing his legs incessantly.

I wasn't sure if he was high or jonesin' but the constant movement was making me crazy. "I'll let you stay here under very strict conditions until your grandpa can pick you up in about three weeks and take you away from here for a while."

"I don't want to go to fuckin' Utah," he yelled.

"That's your choice." It was hard for me to say that. I wanted to wrap him up and take him away from the bullies he had surrounded himself with, like I did when he was a boy. But at nineteen years old and over six foot four, there was really nothing I could do if he didn't want to play by our rules. I was so torn between anger and sadness, I'm not even sure I knew what I felt.

"So wait...let me...so what you're saying is I got to go to Utah or I got to leave."

"Yes. That's what I'm saying."

He jumped out of the chair and spun around, waving his arms and yelling like a child having a tantrum, only larger and scarier with language no child would use. "I ain't fuckin' being treated like a kid, and I ain't fuckin' going to Utah."

"You need to get a hold of yourself and sit back down." Janet spoke for the first time, very calmly.

"What am I supposed to do?" He continued to pace around the room.

"You have a choice to make," I said, gripping the seat of the barstool to keep myself in place.

"Well I ain't staying here and being treated like a twelve-year-old."

"Then you'll need to take your stuff and go." I stood up with some false sense of authority—like I really thought it meant anything. He was a big kid. He could crush me like a bug.

"Fine." He paced, picking up his things and setting them down, and then doing it all over again.

"Remember the offer stands. You can always come back here and stay, but only if you can stay within our boundaries."

"You can stop talking now," he yelled. He finally had all his items in his hands, and as he headed to the door, I followed.

Before I reached him, the door slammed hard behind him, and the whole house shook.

I got home the next day at the same time, and when I came in I locked the door behind me. The house was silent. I sat down on the loveseat in the front room and stared at the door. A few minutes went by before Janet walked in.

"What are you doing?"

"Waiting for the doorbell to ring."

THE BEST PLAN
By Michelle Grubb

The best plan, is no plan.

The best map is the one folded neatly in your back pocket.

The best way to be, is flexible. Not in a Stretch Armstrong kind of way, but in your mind set, your outlook, and in your heart.

I reached thirty before I realised that looking inward wasn't a healthy way forward. For thirty years I missed everything around me where I wasn't the centre of attention. The last twenty years of my life have been amazing; from the moment I figured out I could stand tall, raise my chin, and look beyond my own nose. It's not rocket science, but then, I wasn't building a rocket.

I look up now, not down. Not down at my feet, not down at my phone, and certainly not down on anyone else. I step forward. Not sideways, not backward, and never on top of anyone. When I was thirty, I'd have stepped right through you. Not because you were in my way, but because I would never have seen you. I had me to think about. I had places to go. I had money to make and possessions to accumulate, and I had no time for you, whoever you were.

I've realised ambition is a precarious word balancing on a precarious needle. Tipped one way, ambition is a quality to admire and be admired for. A person with ambition goes places. They strive, they grow, they expand, they strive some more, and they make life happen. Or do they? It's possible a person with ambition—the wrong ambition—is more concerned with the destination rather than the journey.

On the other hand, tipped in the opposite direction, a lack of ambition can lead to a life without a life. I've seen those people, too frightened or too lazy to do anything or go anywhere. Too meek to challenge or be challenged. In my mind, that's a waste of a life that otherwise could have been filled with opportunity. But I can see my ideals are flawed; they may have already reached their destination, or they might be on the journey they have always wanted to be on.

For me, ambition was non-negotiable. I met the right person at the right time and was lucky enough to impress them, in my personal life and my working life. We became lovers. He was married and to this day he remains that way. I learned how to be in love and be single simultaneously, how to lie and be lied to, and ultimately, how to feel worthless.

A tiny whiff of success, and I was on my way to the top. I was one half of a power couple that no one knew existed. It's difficult, juggling your social life around a man with another life entirely. My unpredictable availability to socialise eventually saw my friends dwindle one by one. They were ambitious people, too. I didn't blame them for marching on without me. Just like me, they were on a path to get where they were going.

I've noticed how the people we surround ourselves with can influence how we act, what we say, eat, drink, and ultimately, how we think. It's not a bad thing, but in my twenties, while attracting the affections of an older man, I had nothing to hold on to but how my life appeared from the outside. I wanted the flash car, the big house, the expensive clothes, and the high flying, stressful career. I wanted it all. I'm not painting an unfamiliar story here. In my twenties, I was nothing if not predictable. When I bought the flash car on hire purchase—not the smartest way to spend thirty thousand pounds, and certainly not on a depreciating asset—I later added gold and diamonds. Stupid? Of course. To this day I can't tell the difference between real diamonds and fake ones. I could have saved myself thousands.

You get the picture. I was a self-serving, materialistic twenty-something living in la la land.

So what changed?

When I was twenty-nine, my mother turned sixty. She guilted me into a road trip to celebrate her birthday. For the life of me, I couldn't fathom why anyone would want to celebrate being that old. The thought of spending five days with my mother, trapped in the confines of a comfy family saloon, driving along the south coast of France and into Italy was a hideous notion to say the least. Time out of Britain meant time away from my secret boyfriend, time away from my sparkling clean house, my pristine convertible, and my walk-in wardrobe. Selecting a limited range of outfits for the journey took me nearly a month and almost pushed me toward a breakdown. It was one of the reasons I rarely travelled.

Reality turned out to be far less painful.

There are few people we meet in life who question our ideals, our motives, or our morals. Think about it. We're rarely asked "why?" Not a lame why, like why are you wearing red and not blue. Not that kind of why, but the important, "*Why?*" When was the last time a friend, or foe, asked you why you're doing what you're doing? Why you feel the way you feel? Why you do the things you do? I'd been slowly losing my friends, and my secret boyfriend certainly wasn't about to question my life.

One day I met the person who finally asked that all important question.

Her name is Grace, and she was in her fifties then, like I am now. She had sat across the restaurant from our table in a traditional eatery in Nice. My mother and I weren't conversing. We rarely did. I was trying to message my boyfriend, but he wasn't responding. Mum went to the toilet. Probably not because she needed to, but because she was sick of staring at the top of my head while I stared at my phone.

"Your other mother must be great," Grace said. She smiled warmly. I was confused.

"My other mother?"

"I presume, seeing as though you're ignoring the one you're with, you must have another one. A better one."

I disliked Grace immediately. "I'm busy. I have a busy life. I'm not ignoring her, I'm just getting on with things."

"I hope he's worth it."

Timing is everything, and just at that moment, my mother returned to hear Grace's last comment.

"Who, darling?"

"The man she's messaging," Grace said before I had a chance to think up a lie.

My mother looked from me to Grace. "You didn't tell me about a man."

"That's because I don't have one," I said adamantly.

Grace laughed.

I stared at her.

She raised her eyebrows apologetically at my mother.

The next moment changed my life.

"You're not a very accomplished liar. Especially for someone I imagine has been doing it for some time now."

"Are you lying to me?" Mother asked.

"No," I replied.

Grace coughed.

"Will you just butt out?" I snapped.

Grace looked at my mother and said, "Your daughter is yet to realise that one day, she's going to die. We're all going to die. You, me, the waiter, the chef. Everybody. She hasn't realised life isn't a trial run, and if she fucks this up—excuse my language—she won't get a second chance."

A complete stranger had the audacity to tell me I was mortal, and in front of my ageing mother. Who did this woman think she was?

I looked at my mum, my sixty-year-old mum, who was awkwardly smiling back at me.

"I think she's right," my mother said. "I think you only get one go at this."

In that moment, I realised, one day, I'd be left on earth without her. Alone. I suddenly wanted to turn back time, at least until yesterday when we picked up the car. I wanted to look out the window while she drove so we could chat and admire the scenery together. It occurred to me that I couldn't recall the landscape of an entire day's travel. And I couldn't remember a thing my mother said to me.

The thought of dying, of my mother dying, was terrifying.

This isn't a dress rehearsal.

I switched off my phone.

I saw Grace last week. Unlike me, she isn't afraid of flying so she jumped out of a plane—wearing a parachute, of course. Skydiving is her new hobby. My hobby has been the same since that day in Nice. I look up. I smell the smells. I experience the world. I practice mindfulness. I talk to my mother almost daily, and I love openly with all my heart.

We all end up dead. Buried or cremated, we're dead.

Life is about the journey, not the destination. If there's one predictable thing about life, it's the end.

If you plan to enjoy your life, your map will reveal itself. Let it.

A MOTHER'S LOVE (TOGETHER FOREVER, REMEMBER?)
By Leanne

I write this as a twenty-six-year-old woman, a single parent of a seven-year-old girl. I'm working at a charity full-time, providing support for families who have been affected by domestic abuse. I'm feeling immensely proud of myself, more confident than I've ever been, and bursting with excitement for what my future holds for me.

But then there's that one memory, that one flashback, or the moment I see him in person, and I shake with fear, my hearing goes, and my heart beats faster than ever, leading me to get hot and flustered. After seven years I still can feel myself going back to being a scared young girl, unaware of what's coming at me next.

Here is my story...

When I was twelve, I met my first boyfriend. I was in love and believed we would be together forever. During secondary school, I never made a full day of school. I would always start arguments with family and friends, I was in trouble a lot with the police, and I had to keep up a reputation that he and his family had set–if I didn't, there would be consequences. Growing up as a teenager, I made choices to please him; I put myself in danger and was sexually exploited, but even this didn't stop me loving him.

At first, the relationship was brilliant, and he was the

most loving person I could have hoped to have met. He promised me we'd be together forever, me and him, no matter what. He told me no one else would love me like he did.

On my thirteenth birthday I remember the first time anything physical ever happened. We were arguing in his bedroom, and he started pushing and shoving me around. I was crying and begging for him to stop, but he didn't listen; his voice got louder, and his temper got worse. He slapped me across the face, and we both froze and stared at each other. It was as if he was in shock at what he had done, and I just remember thinking, *oh my God, what is this?*

His mum came upstairs and shouted at him. "Look at her, what have you done? It's her birthday!"

She took me downstairs, and I just cried like a baby. He came down and said sorry. At that point, I should have walked away but I didn't. Together forever, remember?

By the age of fourteen, I was taking drugs and drinking, and he'd started doing all sorts of drugs as well. I went to his friend's house, one with a lot of older guys in it, which would lead to life changing moments for me. I would be encouraged to take drugs, bully people, or even worse, please men to make his life easier. The police eventually became aware of what was going on, and it was all put to a stop. At this point my parents had to be told because of the risk to me. It was only then when my mum started to realise my boyfriend was no good for me. She tried to encourage me to end the relationship, but it would just lead to us arguing. She tried and begged, she encouraged me to speak to workers, but I didn't. Did I make a statement? Did I press charges? Of course I didn't. How could I? The repercussions from my boyfriend and his family didn't seem worth it. So I covered it up, I lied, and I said whatever I could to make sure he wasn't in trouble. Even so, when it was over my boyfriend's friends were punished, and I remained in my relationship despite family and friends begging me to end it. How could I end it? We were going to be together forever, remember?

His temper got worse and by the age of sixteen, I was being physically attacked by him. Still, I loved him and wouldn't leave him. I would be able to tell by his expression, body language, or tone of voice that I was in trouble, and when we were alone, he would punish me for whatever he thought I'd done wrong. I can still feel myself panic and worry every time I think of that "look." I couldn't make full days of school because he wasn't in education at all due to his behaviour, so I would skip school to be with him. He didn't want me being with friends or to see boys without him there. One day, he came to my school and was shouting at me. A friend saw what was going on and tried to help, which led to my partner running out of school, in fear that someone would punish him for the things he was doing to me. When I got home that night from school I got changed and went to his house, even though knew I was going to be in trouble—like every other night.

Somehow, I completed school and my GCSES's, although the grades I got weren't what was expected of me. I started secondary school as a young girl who had a bright future, and I finished it as a scared teenager not knowing how I was ever going to end this. This was the point I probably should have walked away, and looking back now I wish I did, but we were going to be together forever, remember?

I got a job at the age of sixteen as soon as I left school, but again he didn't like me being at work five days a week, with other men, and after a year I left that job. I then went back to college at seventeen, but this didn't help the situation either. He would turn up at college and demand I go to him, and he would threaten boys at the college. I think of all the times he would remove me from college and no one ever helped, no one dared say a word to him. It stuns me no one ever tried to help me. The police were never called, and no one ever asked if I was okay. Although, to be fair, even if they had I wouldn't have told them the truth. How could I get him in trouble? And to be honest, I didn't dare tell anyone what was really happening. After all, he was only doing all of this because he loved me and would do whatever he could to make sure we were together forever, just as he'd promised we would be.

I left my family home and moved in with him just before I turned eighteen in March, 2008. This was following arguments and fights with parents, all about him, and them wanting me to end things with him. But I loved him, and we were going to be together forever, remember?

After we moved in together, things became far worse than I could have imagined. Police were being called out regularly, and I had to attend hospital on numerous occasions due to the beatings I had received. I never pressed charges, and I never made a statement. I couldn't get him in trouble; I loved him, and I knew I would take him back. The beatings were becoming more regular, though, and each time getting that little bit worse. I would hide my bruises or cuts with make up or extra clothing. If someone did ever see them, I'd make up an excuse: "I've tripped on the bath mat," or "I've walked into a door." It was very rare he would make a mark on my face, as he didn't want anyone to know. He was able to manipulate everyone around him to believe he was the kindest, most loving boyfriend.

We'd been together for seven years when, in April 2008, I found out I was pregnant. He promised he would

change and that things would get better between us, so I
decided to keep the baby. I knew I wasn't ready for it, and
I still remember sitting with a friend when I was around
five months pregnant and telling her, "I won't be with him
forever. This won't change him and I'll leave him when I'm
ready."

He kept his word for four months, and things did get
better. Then, the drug addiction got worse, and so did the
beatings. Eventually, my worst fears became reality and the
abuse started leading to sexual assaults—each one more
severe and aggressive. I thought being pregnant would
protect me a little bit, but I was completely wrong. He
knew I would try and protect my baby, and he knew I was
weaker because I was pregnant. I felt worthless and believed
I deserved everything I got. He took all my confidence
away, and he and his family made me believe I was nothing
without them. I couldn't wear makeup or nice clothes and
wasn't allowed out with my friends unless he was with me;
I wasn't allowed to talk to other males, as he would get
jealous. He allowed me to have one friend, because she
played the game and let him think she believed everything
he said. But she would know when something had happened
to me. She used to sit with me until early hours—she was
my safety net.

I remember being in the house one day, and his family
had come to visit us. I was heavily pregnant at the time. I
was in the kitchen wiping something up off the floor, and he
went mad! So as punishment, because he couldn't hit me
with his family there, he picked up the bucket full of bleach
and hot water and tipped it all over me. I just stood in the
kitchen crying, covered in hot, bleachy water.

His uncle came in and said, "Oh Leanne, what have you
done? Pregnancy brain, ay, accidents happen. Go on up and

get changed. I'll sort this mess for you." If only he'd known what had really happened.

I gave birth to my daughter, Sarah, in January 2009. I was in labour for three days, and he only spent four hours with me during that time. My mum was with me constantly throughout, only going home to sleep at night or when he and his family were due to come to see me. Sarah was born late at night on the third, and both he and my mum were there for that. He left twenty minutes after she was born, and to be honest, I was relieved. My mum stayed for hours, as she'd instantly fallen in love with Sarah. After I was discharged from hospital, I arrived back to our home, and he was passed out from drugs on the sofa. When he woke I received my first beating as a mother, in front of my newborn daughter. I sat on my bed after and cried, wondering how I'd gotten to this point, and how I was going to get out. I knew it was time to end the relationship, as I didn't want my daughter seeing this violence, but how could I? Where would I go, who would I tell? Who would dare help me leave him? I was trapped. I simply couldn't see a way out.

By March 2009, social services had become involved due to the risk to my daughter and myself. I was visited regularly by my social worker and health visitor, and I would try and hide my real feelings and put on a front that I was okay. It was very rare I would see these workers alone, because my boyfriend would ensure he attended as many as he could. Then, another beating happened that put me in the hospital again. The social worker came to see me and told me she didn't believe anything I had ever told her, and she told me they were putting my two-month old daughter on a child protection plan. Finally, I was truly able to see the risk to me and Sarah. Social services made the decision to remove my child unless I was able to end the relationship. My social worker rang my mum and asked if she would become my daughter's carer. My mum was very aware of the relationship and what I was going through, although we'd long stopped talking about it.

My mum will tell me she still remembers the day she received that phone call. She begged them not to remove Sarah, because if they did, what more would I have to live for? But they told my mum if I wasn't able to make the right choice, they needed to be able to place Sarah somewhere safe, so obviously my mum agreed. My social worker came to visit me at home, along with my health visitor, and they discussed with me what they were planning to do. At this point I made the decision to end the relationship and began to put a plan in place to keep myself and my daughter safe. I felt so relieved that someone else had made this decision for me.

Before I was able to leave the house (in a safe way) he came home and, surprise, surprise, we had another argument. He got a bottle of bleach, went up to my room, and poured it over every item of clothing in my wardrobe. I think of how devastated I would be if that happened now, but at that point of my life, I felt it was a miracle that he hadn't physically hurt me, and I hadn't packed my clothes, so he wasn't aware I was planning to leave. Had I already packed my belongings, he would have known I was leaving, and what would he have done then? He walked out of the house, leaving behind his phone, keys and belongings, which I took to mean he wasn't coming back. I knew this was the end. I stayed at my Grandma's that night. The next night I returned home. I had to return to prove to myself it was really over. I didn't want to go back to my mum if I thought there would be a part of me that would've taken him back.

I couldn't put my family through what would come next if I didn't intend on following it through. I double checked every door and window was locked, all the curtains were shut, and I only used the bit of light I needed. I didn't want him to know I was there. I kept Sarah downstairs with me, and I sat on the sofa, waiting. He turned up, banged on the doors, begged me to let him in, and tried the door handles and windows. I just laid in silence, cuddling Sarah, counting down the hours until morning so I could get out. The next morning, I packed all our stuff, and I left.

I returned home, nineteen years old and a mother. But in fact, I was a scared, quiet, shy, and anxious little girl. My mum had to mother me like a baby all over again. I needed her more than I had ever needed anyone. Looking back now, returning home was a hard process. We argued, we cried, and I struggled to be without him. He was all I'd known for seven years. Eventually, though, I started opening up to my mum, telling her the truth about what I had gone through. She still doesn't know the full extent of everything, but she knows enough.

He didn't let me go easily. He would follow me, find ways of getting in touch with me, or would send messages. He wouldn't take no for an answer. The thing I remember him saying most is, "You'll never get me out of your life. I will always be here, and no one else will ever be with you because I won't let them. I'll kill for you if I have to."

It started to register that he wasn't bothered about our daughter at all, he was only interested in me. He never asked me, or others, about her. It was always just about me.

As you can imagine, things didn't end there. I finally had the courage to press charges after he assaulted me when I was walking along a street one night. That meant I had to attend various court dates, but I was eventually awarded an injunction against him, and social services decided he couldn't see my daughter any more unless it was supervised. By June 2009 it was agreed that my ex's mum would be the safe person where contact could be arranged. My daughter went to her paternal grandmothers house every Thursday and Sunday, between the hours of two and six pm. He was rarely there, though, which proved that he didn't want her, he just wanted me. I actually started to believe he would never let me go, that I would never be free from him, and I would never have a normal life.

This continued up to Christmas 2009, when he kicked off on Boxing Day because things hadn't gone his way. I decided it wasn't safe for my daughter to be left with them for the day and told his mum I would be in contact to rearrange. I reported my ex-partner for what had happened, and he was arrested and taken to court for his offences. Unfortunately, this caused arguments between me and his family and they stopped answering my calls, never turned up for meetings with social care, and never got in touch to resume contact with my daughter. This led social services to make the decision, along with myself, that if my ex-partner wanted to resume contact, he would have to take me to court. Social services were involved from the time she was born and stayed in contact with me to help until she was one. They have always stood by their decisions and helped me as best they could.

I was supported by a member of staff at NIDAS throughout the court hearings. The staff worker encouraged me to receive further support, but I wouldn't engage with the worker—despite them making various attempts. But I worked closely with my social worker and received help where and when needed. Ultimately, I didn't want to admit to what I had allowed myself to go through or have a daughter born into. Hiding it away at the time seemed like the best coping mechanism. Finally, however, I started to receive real support about a year later when those coping mechanisms failed.

It turns out, we weren't going to be together forever. He didn't love me and care for me like no one else did. He just wanted me to believe that, so I depended on him and would never leave him. But the truth is far better; without him, I can actually see a future that doesn't include pain and fear.

It's now 2016, and I have completely transformed my life for the sake of myself and my daughter. I am now happy, confident, and content in myself. I've never been in such a happy place. My daughter is in full time school and has no involvement with social services. She has grown to be a happy, content, and loving little girl. Contact has never gone ahead, although every now and again my ex-partner will send a note to a friend's house threatening to take me to court. I don't think he'll ever stop trying to intimidate me, and I know how to manage the situation better now; I'm aware of what support is available and how I can access it when it's needed.

I believe everything happens for a reason, and I believe this happened to enable me to help others in this situation and to be a mum to the most amazing, incredible little girl. She is the light at the end of my tunnel, she's my best friend, and she's my angel. She saved me from a life of abuse and punishment. Everything I do is for Sarah, and even though sometimes I struggle, she's worth every moment. I know when Sarah is older I'll have some hard questions to answer about her dad and what happened. One thing I can always promise her is everything I have ever done has always been for her and always will be. She will know the truth when she is old enough to understand, but at seven years old all she needs to know is that she did have a mummy and daddy who loved each other, but the love we shared wasn't safe. But no matter what, she'll forever have a mummy who loves her, infinity times infinity.

FEARLESSLY FAITHFUL
By Ellen Storey

As a child I only saw my maternal grandmother once a year when we travelled to Bavaria to see her and my grandad for the summer holidays. They lived in a small fifth floor flat in a rural part of Regensburg, and although it was often deathly dull for us as children to be cooped up there for five weeks at a time, I enjoyed the peace of the place, which contrasted greatly with my British home.

The enduring image of my "Oma"(grandma Josefine) is her short, rotund frame, mostly wrapped in an apron, and with stockinged feet curled up on the couch, chatting, chewing her nails, or softly snoring, resignation written across her features. Her grey hair was always neatly coiffured, pinned, and covered with a fine net, and chunky spectacles masked red, watery eyes. I didn't understand a lot of what she said, as my German back then was as basic as her Sudeten German dialect was broad, but her tone of voice and face were very expressive, and it was easy to discern her mood. She would raise her voice to lament various issues but often run out of breath mid-moan. I don't recall her ever complaining about "Papa," her inflexible, conservative husband who insisted on lunch being served at precisely midday, and dinner at six p.m. As far as I could see, she had no life beyond serving him. He saw the telephone as a means to fix appointments and discouraged her from using it to chat. He went out for a walk each day in the woods, but she wasn't fit enough to accompany him. He didn't seem to engage in any kind of meaningful conversation with her, preferring to read the paper, watch TV with his headphones on, or play chess/cards with his grandchildren when we stayed there. Meanwhile, Oma was the dutiful carer, cooking beautiful nutritious meals, ensuring he took his tablets, washing his back in the bath, and protecting his peace (his heart condition made him cry out in pain on a regular basis, and they both had a siesta every afternoon).

Oma's resentment at her fate had to vent in other ways. She couldn't resist nagging her grandchildren in the name of decency, and whilst her relatives mocked her for this, I felt her vulnerability intensely. She would wag her trembling arthritic finger for extra effect as she scolded us, apparently outraged at our lack of morals, as though we couldn't possibly be descended from her. We were reprimanded for countless misdemeanours, including giggling helplessly during the never-ending, monotonous grace my grandparents chanted due to the word *Vater* which broke the intolerable tension at the dinner table, usually only punctuated by what I saw as our grandparents' soup-slurping competitions.

I loved the mixed spice aroma of Oma's tiny carpeted kitchen even when she wasn't cooking. I enjoyed watching her knead dumplings with soft, freckly hands, or sampling delicious soup from a shaky ladle, and the edible atmosphere she created with bacon, goulasch, melting butter and onions, parsley, cucumber salad, cinnamon, chocolate marble cake...those smells still evoke warm memories. We always said she should open her own restaurant, but she was very modest about her gourmet, beautifully presented cuisine murmuring, *wenn's nur schmeckt*, (as long as you like it) without lifting her eyes from her plate.

On the rare occasions that relatives visited, she became very animated as though she felt the need to be the entertainer. Sometimes she would sing for guests, with her brother accompanying her on the accordion occasionally, and her heavy vibrato was poignant to listen to. Sometimes I thought I saw tears when she looked into my eyes; who knows, maybe her *Schatzele* (little treasure) reminded her in some way of the beloved daughter she'd lost many years before.

It was only three years after she died that I began editing my mother's memoirs of the expulsion of Germans from Eastern Europe following World War Two, and a very different "Pepi" (Josefine) emerged—bold, vivacious, heroic, independent. She was born just after the turn of the twentieth century in what was formerly Saaz in Bohemia, a part of the Sudetenland which is now Zatec in the Czech Republic. Hers was a large middle class family with many cultural interests and musical gifts, and her father played cello in a theatre orchestra in his spare time. A tomboy with an unbridled appetite for adventure—she once nearly drowned trying to fish an item of interest out of a river; it was only her large frilly underwear trapping air which allowed her to float—she was subject to sanctions such as kneeling in the corner or being chained to an object outside. None of these subdued her lively spirit.

As a young woman, Pepi adored brass bands, Strauss waltzes, operettas, silent movies, amateur dramatics, singing in music halls, and of course dancing and partying— sometimes staying out all night during carnivals, dashing home only to bathe before going straight on to work. She was skilled in needlework and longed to be a seamstress, but ended up taking over her sister's hairdressing business after the latter got married in 1918, a job which once involved accompanying a client to a Hungarian spa for five weeks. A popular girl with black hair and a sense of fun, embracing the rapidly changing world of machinery, electricity, and visible legs as a woman, but she had no interest in maintaining elegant appearances, unlike her mother and sisters, and preferred the company of her equally ludic younger brother.

She had a peculiar manner of selecting, or deselecting, her love interests—one hapless man was rejected on account of having odd socks. Another more serious suitor invited Pepi to emigrate with him to Bogota, but she declined, feeling a responsibility towards her mother who was now frail. Another romance ended when the man bought her an engagement ring and then abruptly disappeared to Vienna with no word of explanation.

She was thirty when she met Nand (Ferdinand), a man seven years her junior, and from farming stock. It would seem she felt more compassion than passion for him. He was unemployed, and life had become much harder for Germans in what was now Czechoslovakia, following the end of WWI and the fall of the Austro-Hungarian Empire. Nand was often pursued and even beaten by Czech militia for his nationality and political leanings. They married in 1931 despite her mother's frantic protests—"He's a child and a peasant, you have nothing in common!"—and Nand went to live with Pepi and his new mother-in-law. Pepi carried on her hairdressing part-time for six years whilst Nand was out of work doing odd jobs and unwaged labour which was humiliating for him. After the birth of their first child in 1932, she would hurry home between jobs to breastfeed and even nursed other infants in exchange for payment. Pepi's mother died, and she found herself working doubly hard to maintain a home, income, and family, with their second daughter, my mother, born in 1936. She was also battling Nand's chauvinism and her own secret regret at marrying him.

Her younger daughter Erika, my mother, was jealous of her sister Liesl, who was clearly the favourite. She received special care from Pepi and medical attention on account of her heart condition, which caused respiratory problems and made her lips and nails blue. Pepi made endless sacrifices for her treasured Liesl, even carrying her to school during a period of sickness for three weeks at her behest. Liesl prized learning and objected to staying home ill. Erika would refuse her mother's food to divert attention and avenge herself, but Pepi got wise and sent meals to the neighbours, where she would eat them with gusto.

In 1943, Nand was drafted to work on the railways and ended up as a PoW overseas for two years. When the war was finally lost and the systematic persecution and starvation of Germans began, Pepi's home remained open for people to come and find solace and hospitality. As stateless German refugees poured into the area from East Prussia and Silesia, Pepi was one of those to offer refuge, and they slept cheek to jowel with no floor space in the flat. Bombing raids created terror, and Pepi and her family watched the red night glow of Dresden burning less than a hundred miles away. Rumours that the Russian Army were fast approaching evoked terror and many committed suicide, including her neighbours.

On 10th May 1945, the hammer fell as Soviet troops from Mongolia arrived on horseback and began raiding with machine guns, raping day and night, making no female over twelve and under seventy safe. Their other hobbies were drinking, dancing, and campfires which rendered sleep impossible. There were two attractive teenage twins in the building who were constantly pursued, and one night they came breathless to Pepi to seek refuge in their flat. She told them to hide behind my mother's bed and hastily threw a feather bed over them. Shortly after, the familiar hammer on the door with machine guns made everyone jump, and Pepi opened up to two soldiers who barged in and began their hunt for the girls, stepping over refugees lying on the floor and using torches to look under bedclothes and in wardrobes. As they neared my mum's bed, Pepi suddenly exploded and grabbed one soldier by the arm, herding them through the kitchen and pushing them so hard out of the front door they almost fell over each other. It was at these moments that her formerly criticised fearlessness came in very useful.

In June of 1945, Czech officials announced that the family had ten minutes to pack their belongings in order to be transferred to a local barracks. The ever-resourceful Pepi had sewn cash into her suspender belt. She used it to escape the camp by paying a lorry driver to take them to East Germany where they found shelter at another camp. She fought to get Liesl, who was gravely ill through malnourishment, into a hospital for six months whilst she did odd jobs, including cleaning the camp toilets and sewing for the Camp Commandant's wife for token money. Her stance was that she would rather they starve to death than beg, but this meant working six days a week and enduring abuse from her employers, whilst trying to find time to visit her daughter in hospital. Eventually she'd saved enough to rent a very basic room for herself and Erika, who was relieved to escape the camp with its dismal watery soup and scarce food provided by aid agencies. Initially, they used a cart to transport firewood from a nearby forest, but this soon dried up, and they were often huddled together to keep warm.

Pepi, a devout Catholic, began going to church again with Erika, and a congregation member gave them a Bible and prayer book which they read from every day. Although food was rationed and inadequate, they finally had a sense of freedom and hope that their luck would turn, especially when Erika returned to school, and Nand returned briefly, directed by the Red Cross, to urge them to join him in West Germany where his parents now lived. They had no papers and would therefore have to go illegally, the plan being to cross the border near Hof, formerly on the boundary of East and West Germany and now the border of Czech Republic and Germany. Nand would meet Pepi and the girls on the other side, but they would have a male companion, who was also hoping to re-join family in the West, and this reassured my grandfather. As they were crossing the border however, shots rang out and their companion disappeared into nearby trees temporarily, while Pepi marched on resolutely with her girls. Fearless!

Eventually they settled in Regensburg, but Liesl's health had now greatly deteriorated and heart valve surgery was not an option at that time. She died aged seventeen, and this no doubt broke Pepi. Her eyesight was badly affected for some time after, as though she couldn't face reality, but her faith remained strong. The morning after she woke up from a dream in which she'd seen Liesl floating above telegraph wires like an angel. The vision rendered her euphoric.

Mother Nature prepared my Oma well for death. Perhaps she'd been ready far longer than we knew. Her pleasures and occupations in life gradually fell away one by one. Previously she had crocheted bandages for overseas lepers to protect their withered limbs from hungry vermin. It was a chance to share her boundless love with a helpless world from the comfort of her sofa. She still played games occasionally, although the last time I played draughts with her, aged ten, it was clear that her mind was no longer up to the job. The counters in her hand began to float any which way, and when I protested, my mother hastily hushed me. Soon, precious few occupations or rewards remained; Mon Cheri chocolates (my sister couldn't resist raiding the secret stash she thought we knew nothing about), magazine crosswords, cooking, Dallas, Dynasty.

My grandad took any impetus she had with him when he died of a heart attack in 1990. "Der arme, Papa," she would say wistfully, but in reality she was the "poor" one. She begged to be taken to live in the UK, and this induced some guilt in my mother who had to refuse, even though she travelled to visit her at every opportunity. She found her an immaculate nursing home in the countryside, but Oma resented the fact it was gobbling up the savings she'd foregone so long during her mostly frugal life. She suffered a stroke as well as boredom and loneliness. Her decades of isolation had left her bereft of social skills, and she gave up, asking us repeatedly on the phone to pray for God to "take her away." The two-year wait was long for her.

For many years I believed that all elderly people must be unhappy by default. I always saw my grandmother as pitiful when she was alive, but the truth was she just chose to give her power away to those she felt needed it more. She put others before herself without thinking, in true Christian style. But she neglected to love herself too and became a martyr. It's a mystery as to why she apparently didn't feel worthy of true happiness, when she'd more than earned it over the years. I suspect it was the thought of her ultimate destiny that sustained her through the wilderness years.

SUBJECT MATTER EXPERT
By Wendy May

"I really don't think I can do this," I said to Cassandra as I tapped my fingers on the desk impatiently.

"You'll be fine, Amy. It'll be over in a flash."

I scoffed and swung my chair back to face the monitor, shaking my head. "Then why do it at all? I can just email it to them. Or maybe one of the guys can do it. They normally do these briefings." I gave her a pleading look over my shoulder.

"Finish it, and then we'll do a practice run. Just you and me, okay?" Cassandra rolled her chair back to her workstation. "Anyway, it's good that you're doing this. Last survey said there were less than twenty percent women working here. It doesn't hurt to stand up and be seen sometimes."

I nodded reluctantly and continued to type, adding the all-important take-home message. *There.* It seems good on paper but me, standing up, briefing Senior Military Members and the Director of an Intelligence Agency? *There's no way I can carry this off.*

Later, the afternoon sun streamed into the conference room and made me uncomfortably warm. I nudged the lectern with my high-heeled shoe as I waited.

"That was good, but try it again, with more... conviction. You're the subject matter expert after all, not them. They might be Management, but they don't do your job. They need you to tell them what you know," Cassandra said from the back row.

I dropped my dog-eared page on the ledge, tucked my hair back behind my ears, and tried to stand up straighter behind the polished wood lectern. I looked up to see her expectant face. Her hands were clasped in her lap as she gave me her full attention. I couldn't help but stifle a laugh at my faithful colleague. She wouldn't let me tackle this unprepared.

"Good Morning Director, Senior Managers, Ladies, and Gentlemen," I began again.

Fifteen minutes later, much to my embarrassment, Cassandra stood up and clapped. Good thing we'd shut the conference room door or half the office would think they'd missed a show.

"That was much better. Do that tomorrow, okay? You can do this," she said with a self-satisfied grin.

I drove home that evening, dreading the morning to come. My hands were clammy on the wheel, and there was still over twelve hours to go. Would I get any sleep at all?

The next day, and after virtually no sleep, the morning traffic was slow, and I had to park miles away from my building. The last thing I needed was to be all hot and flustered before my briefing. No time for coffee, let alone breakfast.

"Morning!" Cassandra said, strategically ignoring my red face and slightly hassled demeanour.

A coffee cup sat on my desk, steam drifting out of the small hole in the lid. "You're an angel. Thank you, Cass." I gripped the cup as though it might contain some sort of anti-anxiety potion.

"I'm getting there early so I can get a good seat."

"Oh God."

"Drink! Don't think too much. You'll be fine, I promise," Cassandra said with certainty.

I had no option but to follow her instructions and read through my briefing one last time. My feet and hands were cold now, and my heart was racing. I could feel the tension getting worse, but I was determined to get through this somehow. My computer chimed. Fifteen minutes. *Okay, that gives me enough time to go to the bathroom at least twice.* "Cass, do you know when I'm on?"

"First," she said.

"What!" That was either really cruel or good fortune. I decided on good fortune; get it over and done with quickly.

Cassandra stood and put her tailored black jacket on. "I'm going to go, I'll see you there. Remember, conviction!" Cassandra punched the air with her small hand as she left the workspace and headed for the conference room.

Ten minutes later, I glanced at my favourite chair in the back row and reluctantly continued walking to the front of the conference room. My hands were shaking as I sat in the front row alongside the Director and several senior Military and Civilian Managers. I tried to focus on the well-dressed host as he introduced himself, making a mental note to remember to do the same. I looked down at my crumpled page of notes. Fifteen minutes, and it will be over. *I'm the subject matter expert. Say it with conviction.*

I took my place behind the lectern. "Good Morning, Director, Senior Managers, Ladies, and Gentlemen." I chanced a quick look out across the sea of faces. Two hundred men and women, some familiar, some I'd never seen before. The pointed toe of my best shoes tapped nervously behind the lectern, but they couldn't see that. Neither could the other ninety interstate staff connected via the live video link. I spotted Cassandra's beaming face in the second row. Swallowing dryly, I quickly looked back to my notes.

"My name is Amy Carlsen." *Deep breath. Don't pass out.* "Today I'd like to brief you on the current situation."

I went on, somewhat unsteadily. I looked up again. Along with all the men in the room, the female Director and two female Senior Managers were nodding as I spoke. Occasionally one would smile and take notes. They were listening to me. To me, up there, talking to them.

Cassandra was the first to start clapping at the end of my briefing. But this was quickly followed by several questions from the Director, which sparked a discussion amongst the rest of the staff in the room. I was still standing up the front, but now, I wasn't hiding behind the lectern. I was involved in the discussion as questions were directed back to me. And I had the answers, because I was the subject matter expert.

Before returning to my seat in the front row, I finally smiled back at Cassandra.

STRONG ENOUGH
By L.C.

The first time I had to go to court was on a bright spring morning in March.

I woke up, and I knew it was a big day. I knew that I had to be strong, otherwise he would get away with everything and do it all again to someone else, or maybe worse.

It was my time. I had to look innocent, so I was wearing a dress which looked like a dress you'd wear to go to church on Sunday. It had blue spots inside white spots on a turquoise background. Once I stepped in the room where I'd be talking to the judge, I realised that they wouldn't even see my dress. All they would be able to see was from my waist up. But before I sat down I would have to say an oath. I can't remember the oath, but I remember looking at my councillor because I felt silly.

I needed someone to be with me, other than my mum. You know, like a friend who makes me laugh. So my friend Zoe came with me and brought a giant box of loom bands, because she knew that they would keep my mind calm.

Once we arrived I was so nervous. I didn't know whether he'd get away with it. But that was only something I'd find out later. I was waiting for the court to be all set up and ready for me, but before I had to go in, I had to go through all of my police statements about him breaking the restraining order. I couldn't talk about it to my mum because mum was a witness too, as was one of my neighbours. While waiting, I had plenty of time to think about the reason we were all there. About how he'd broken the restraining order, and how I just wanted it all to stop.

B and I had been dating for nine months. The first two months were wonderful. I wouldn't have wanted anyone else. After we slept together though, it got harder. I found out I was pregnant two months after. I stole a pregnancy test and found out in Weatherspoons. I was thirteen. It took me another week to make a decision about what to do. It was terrifying. I decided not to have it, because I thought my mum would move me away from all my friends and family, and it scared me. I was being naughty before that, out drinking and messing around, so I knew she wouldn't understand. I made the decision not to have it, but I didn't tell her. I went to the doctor with my boyfriend's family instead to figure out what to do. The doctor asked why I was getting rid of it—I wasn't old enough. I wasn't ready.

After the abortion, my boyfriend no longer saw me as his girlfriend, but rather as someone who killed his child. We both wanted to keep it, really, but I knew he'd get in trouble because he was fifteen. He isolated me, kept me from seeing my friends, and started screaming and shouting at me. The abuse became physical. I was always covered in bruises, and he eventually gave me internal bruising on my ribs. I didn't tell anyone. The one best friend I had, abandoned me for my boyfriend's best friend. I didn't tell anyone else, because I convinced myself we were just playing rough, and I bruised easily. I told myself it wasn't his fault.

One day, he thought I was supposed to meet him somewhere, but I'd told him I was going home. He called and told me we were over, that he didn't want to see me ever again. By that time, I didn't care anymore. We were breaking up all the time, so it really didn't matter. I went out with a friend to a snooker club and met someone else while we were out. The next day, I went home, and my boyfriend was on my street, waiting for me. We went back and forth, talking about getting back together. B told me he still loved me, that he still wanted to be with me. But at that point, I knew I was really done with him. He'd been awful, and I didn't want to be with him anymore.

I called James, the guy I'd been with the night before, and we agreed to meet. On my way out, B showed up to try and convince me we should get back together. I told him no, that I wanted nothing to do with him. It was weird; I could actually see the change in him. One minute he was crying, the next he was raging. He put his arm against my throat and pinned me to the wall. He let me go and picked up my little Pomeranian to hurt her. He took off with the dog, and I called my mum, panicking. She called B and went and got the dog. She told me to go home because I had school tomorrow.

That was the first true moment of violence. At least, the first one I really acknowledged as such.

I kept seeing both James and B, unsure who I wanted to be with. It was a massive rollercoaster emotionally, and I started cutting myself. It helped calm me down in some strange way.

B's behaviour got worse. He started stalking me, smashing my windows, threatening my friends and family. At one point, he went after James, and the three of us got into a horrible physical confrontation. My mum came out of the house with a pole and told him to stay away from us. We were truly finished, and I just wanted him to go away.

On 28th Dec 2014, B was outside the house, banging on the door, demanding gifts be returned. From that day, it was a constant problem. I wasn't scared, as much as I was angry. I wanted it to stop and for him to go away. He'd threatened my friends, so I had no one to hang out with. I was so alone. The police gave him a warning to stay away from me, but he went online and sent a topless photo of me to all my friends. I couldn't face going back to school. We went to the police and filed a restraining order.

In February, the restraining order became official. Not long after, he ignored it and showed up at my house He kept coming into our garden and banging on my bedroom window. He simply wouldn't go away.

That led to my first time in court to talk about him breaking the restraining order. He had to wear a tag and stay away from me, but I knew it wasn't going to work, that it wouldn't stop him. I wanted him in prison, but they wouldn't do it because of his age. The lawyer was saying that B was never at my house, trying to get in, and even if he was, my story suggested that I wanted him there. He tried to make me out as someone I'm not, and it made me so furious.

And I was right. Even with the tag on, he came and set fire to the shed against my house. But we couldn't prove it. The fire brigade said it was petrol bombed, and another petrol bomb was thrown at my grandparent's house. He kept calling, saying he was going to burn down the house, and told my mum she'd better watch me, otherwise they'd find me dead on the front lawn. He was terrorising me and my family. It was awful. The police suggested I didn't go to school because it wasn't safe. It messed up my GCSEs.

He left me alone for about two weeks, but I was constantly waiting for the next thing to happen. I was out with some friends one night, and B was in the area. The boy I was with kissed me, and I was so filled with rage at B that I didn't care that it would set him off. On the way home, we passed some pitch dark fields, and I had no idea B was behind me the whole way, until I turned to find he and his friends close enough to hurt us, and I saw a knife blade glinting in his hand. I pulled my friend behind me to try and protect him, and B threatened to stab me. Instead though, he handed the knife to his friend and punched me in the face.

I was in shock. I couldn't have imagined he'd do something like that. Even though he'd been violent before, he'd never simply attacked me that way. He went to punch my friend, and I kicked him in the crotch. "Fuck off. You've split my lip open." That's what I tried to say, anyway. Given the damage he'd done to my face, it probably didn't sound like that. He and his friends ran off, leaving me bleeding and numb.

I called my mum and told her we needed to go to A&E. My friend was panicking and kept trying to catch the blood to put it back in my lip.

After I got my stitches, B was arrested. One of the police officers who'd been dealing with the stalking came to the house and said we were going to do a video recording of the abuse and violence. It took about thirty minutes to tell everything that had happened. I refused to be afraid or to cry. I was strong and wasn't going to let him get to me. Until, that is, he told his youth worker that he was going to kill me. Then I couldn't walk past the area where he'd punched me anymore, and I was afraid to go out at night. Suddenly, the threats and violence felt very real.

That led to the second court date, and the day we had to be in court, I woke up knowing that I couldn't make myself look better, the way I usually do. I was wearing my school clothes to make me look like a normal girl, but my lip was still swollen and make-up couldn't hide the stitches or bruising.

We sat at the court house, waiting. It took until half ten to find out that the prison had sent him to the wrong court, and we had to wait till he was there. At twelve o'clock he had arrived at the right court, but wasn't ready yet, and they told us it would be best for us to go to get some dinner, so we went to McDonalds and ate slowly, because we had an hour and fifteen minutes to kill time. I hated sitting there waiting. I couldn't have a cigarette, and I was getting really wound up. I just wanted it to be over.

Once we got back, one of the witnesses didn't have to come back in. Her name was Louise, and she was B's youth worker. B had told Louise that he was going to kill me if he went down for punching me in the face. So Louise didn't have to come in after all. He pleaded guilty for saying that but not for punching me in the face.

I walked into the same room as the time before, but obviously I wasn't as nervous as last time, because it was my second time being there. I hated it so much because they asked me what happened, and I told them that B punched me in the face and made my tooth puncture my lip, which led me to having ten stitches; six on the outside, four on the inside. They decided that they were going to play the video of me telling them about him punching me, which was taken one day after I had my stitches put in.

So I sat there for half an hour, just listening to myself slurping and sucking in my spit so I didn't dribble everywhere. B's defender tried to turn everything I said back around on me. For example, when I said that there was no street light, the defender tried to say that I wouldn't know it was him if it was dark, but in the end, after tearing up and getting really angry, the defender finally stopped interrogating me. I was already upset because I didn't realize how stupid I sounded with my stitches in it; it made me feel like everyone was laughing at me.

I saw my friend walk into the same room I'd been in. Later, I found out that he was only in there for fifteen minutes, when I'd been in there for fifty minutes. He was there because he was my boyfriend at the time, and that's why B came after us. He was providing more testimony, though I hadn't known he was going to.

The prosecutor was trying to make sure I would win the case, but the defender was really pushing my buttons. I described everything, but because B had a balaclava on the night he punched me, they said I wouldn't be able to identify him. How stupid. Of course I could identify him. I'd spent the last year seeing him almost every day. I knew his eyes, and I obviously knew his voice. I wish I could have told the defender to fuck off and shut the fuck up, but to be honest, if I did that I would have been told off.

The next day, B was found guilty and was sent to prison for two years.

And then...there was a final court date. That was because he made a fake profile of me and posted all of the pictures he'd taken of me in my underwear. A friend of mine told me about it, and we rang the police to report it. I knew that B was in prison for two years, one year with good behaviour, but they pulled out another case against him from me. I didn't have to wait long for this one, and once again, I felt like a pro at being at court. This case was about inappropriate pictures of me that he had taken. Some I knew about, others I didn't. The prosecutor knew that the defender couldn't really say much about this one, and I wasn't there that long before I was able to go home. He didn't get any extra time in prison, but he has to be on the sex offenders list for five years after he comes out of prison.

He also has to have his internet checked for seven years.

Since B has been in prison, I have finally been able to live my life, but there have been problems with anxiety, paranoia, and depression because of the abortion I had one August 2014, but other than that, I've turned my life around and found the best boyfriend I could ask for, and he makes me so happy. Me and my mum get along better now, but I am worried about when B gets out of prison, because I have no idea whether my future is going to be the same as my past. I hope not.

You know, if I could turn back time to change anything, guess what? I fucking wouldn't. I'm happy that I went against him, because it has made me the strong person I need to be. The person I am now, I am because I had to go through something really awful. But I found out I was strong enough to get through it.

If I had to say anything to someone going through the same thing, I'd tell them that if they've got a chance to fight, not to turn it down. It will come back to the bad people eventually. There's no point living in fear if you don't have to. And you don't have to, for any reason at all. There's always going to be someone there to fight beside you. You just have to find the right people. They're out there.

Names have been changed for privacy reasons

Junk Mail
By Leah Johnson

I felt a sharp stabbing pain in my eyes as I was awakened by the light blazing in through the window. I became aware that I'd spent last night passed out on the floor in the front room of the house were I'd been staying.

I knelt down on the carpet and began to look for the foil and wrap from last night. I wanted to see if there was anything left. My fingers clawed desperately at the thin carpet so much that the nylon came off and rolled tight under my fingernails. I managed to find some spare change on the floor and a lighter that still worked, but nothing else.

The money wasn't enough for my bus fare to go and sign on with.

I wondered if it was worth me searching the bedroom, but I didn't want to risk disturbing him. It's better for me if he stays asleep. One good thing about him doing too much smack is that I don't have to lie there and pretend I'm enjoying it.

I expect he's taken it all. That's why he's still in bed and can't get up.

I became aware that my body ached and a chill ran down my back, but my palms were sweaty. My long thick hair was stuck to my face with sweat. I scooped it up and tied it back loosely with a hair ruffle from around my wrist.

It was then I noticed the marks around my arm. Bruises

reminded me of last night's scuffle, where he'd held me down with both hands. I vaguely remember arguing about money and whether or not I'd been seeing someone else. He'd told me that he'd paid off what he owed on the car. But last night they'd rung and I took the call.

"He hasn't paid up yet."

"He's not here right now. Ring back later," I said.

"It's no good you telling me that. It's nothing to do with you. He thinks he can get away with it. Don't make me wait. Deal with it!"

"Just give me a little bit of time," I said.

I hung up. That was the start of last night's fight.

I needed to get my dole money today, as it would help with the money I had to somehow get. I can't get my giro by post anymore because I'm on NFA (No Fixed Abode), which means I don't have an address to post it to. Instead, I have to wait in the dole queue for NFA claimants to sign on, and then come back again two days later to queue again for Personal Issue payouts. This can be tiresome, and it's also one of the places where Gary used to come to see me. He knew I'd be there.

I don't have a job anymore, because I can't get a job without an address. I can't use the address where I'm staying as it fucks his claim up. Not that I can hold a job down now anyway, I have far too much shit going on in my life.

My head pounded as I closed my eyes to try to forget the accumulation of problems weighing me down.

I've been staying here for a few years now. It all started when I left my parent's house after a row. I was young when I'd met Gary in a bar where I was working. I didn't really like him. My instincts told me to stay away from him and not to get involved, but as he was a regular and I was a barmaid, I was obliged to chat.

I felt low at the time, and soon I believed he was the only person I could go to. Gary's older than me, and he's good at manipulating situations. He used my past to get inside my mind. The longer I've stayed here with him, the more cut off I've become from my family. If the phone rings for me and I chat to one of my friends it would cause that much trouble and violence, it just wasn't worth me having the call.

Now I'm trapped in a relationship built entirely on denial and dependency.

I've not spoken to my Dad for a year now, and when I try to call him from the landline, the phone just rings dead. Gary reckons that my Dad has moved, and he doesn't want to tell me where. I've made several attempts to leave him, but they've all ended badly. Most days I convince myself that I want to be here, and this is what I want my life to be, but deep down I know really it's not. If I stay here for much longer, I know I'll never get what I want in my life. This will be it, forever.

Sitting on the carpet, bruised and exhausted, I decide to try and leave him again. I could take the car and drive it to my Dad's just to see if he still lives there. I hear a thud and the letterbox rattle. I jump slightly as the mail lands on the floor. I notice that a pile of unopened junk mail has been accumulating on the front door mat.

I decide to flip through some of the letters in the heap, for no particular reason. I notice a court summons addressed to him. I open it, non-payment of car speeding fine, driving with no insurance, careless driving, and possession of Class A drugs with intent to supply. Now incurring a higher penalty, due to no responses and no appearances made at magistrates court on date of hearing.

That explains why he doesn't want to drive the car

anymore. He's been pulled, and he didn't bother to tell me.

I take the letters and shove them in a kitchen drawer with the lighter and spare change. I leave the mountain of junk mail in front of the door.

Then suddenly I hear the handle on the front door click downwards. I realise that the door is unlocked as someone tries to open it, but the door gets stuck in the big pile of unread mail. This gives me time to react. The man didn't even bother to try to knock, which can't be a good thing, so I try to kick the door shut, but he puts his foot in the doorway to prevent it from closing. I trap his foot in the door and notice that his shoes were Oxford style. Not the footwear I was expecting. I stamp on his foot as hard as I can. He yelps and slowly I let him withdraw his foot, then I slam the door shut using my body weight as I fling my shoulders into the door. I hold the door closed with all the strength I have, pressing hard against the glass, while I turn the key in the lock.

Thank God for junk mail.

Attempting to leave now is out of the question. The man in the Oxford shoes will probably be hanging around outside, which means I can't get my dole money either.

I waited until later, peeking through the curtains until the bloke left. Gary was still asleep upstairs. I pushed the car off the drive without starting the engine, so he won't hear me go. I made that mistake last time I tried to leave. I knew I needed to drive carefully or else I'd get caught. This car has already been pulled with serious offences attached. I'll get to my dad's then dump the car somewhere else.

When the car was down the street, I climbed in, and started the engine. I turned left onto Farnborough road, and half way down the hill I looked in my front mirror and noticed a light blue estate car with a male driver coming up fast behind me.

I put my foot down on the gas, but the car kept on speeding up and remained right up close to my back bumper. If I braked, the car would've crashed right into the back of me. I can't drive to Dad's now. I don't want anyone following me.

Instead I decided to drive in the opposite direction. I did a handbrake turn on the left onto South Church Drive. I screeched around the corner then raced up the hill. I jumped two sets of traffic lights on the way up, because I knew I couldn't stop. I came to a zebra crossing, and I knew that the people who were waiting to cross couldn't see me coming due to the brow of the hill causing a blind spot for oncoming traffic. But if I stopped now, the impact from him running into the back of me would push me forward into the pedestrians. So I had to make a sudden turn in the road.

I pulled up quickly, slammed my brakes, and stopped on the other side of the road. Fortunately, there wasn't anything coming in the opposite direction. Everyone waiting at the crossing stared at me. He braked too. The moment hit me with a prolonged intensity. My mind felt erratic, and I noticed my hands were shaking whilst gripping the wheel. I took longer and deeper breaths to try and calm my anxiety.

The people at the zebra crossing waited and watched to see what would happen next before they decided to cross the road. They soon chose to carry on with their normal lives without getting involved in mine.

I rested my head on the wheel as I felt the world spinning around me. I wished I was one of the pedestrians at the crossing, getting on with a normal life, and not the girl trapped behind the wheel of a stolen car and being chased by some wanker who's either a dealer or a copper. I don't want to feel like the girl who's too scared to get out of the car in case she gets her head kicked in or arrested for a serious offence, which she hasn't committed. I decided to park up, down the side street next to the shops, close to the crossing and to the crowd of people coming back from work doing their shopping. He followed me, parking across the street from me. I opened the car door because I had to get out. There was no point in sitting in the car, waiting. He did the same. He was wearing a suit. I glanced at his feet, and I saw his Oxford shoes.

He never spoke to me. I think he was shocked to see that I was alone in the car, as he was expecting to see me with Gary. It was at this moment that I became aware that *I* was the payment, not the car. The "car debt" was probably a drug debt. Gary had been conspiring with Oxford Shoes. I'd seen them talking on the drive a few days ago when I'd looked out of the window. Oxford Shoes sometimes came and parked around the corner and sat in his car waiting and watching the house. I'd also seen them swapping and driving each other's cars. When I asked Gary who he was and what he wanted, he said he was just somebody who wanted to buy some Class A's. Women are often redefined by men, and Oxford Shoes was a man who needed to keep his integrity, so I became a Class A drug.

Oxford Shoes did speak to me once, a while back. He knocked on the door when Gary was busy in the garage. He told me he was solicitor, and he asked me if the car was in my name. I didn't comment. He told me not to worry about the criminal charges, since the speeding fine was a small amount and the possession charge could be lifted. I knew the charges were more serious than that, and I didn't believe he was a solicitor. All I knew was that the criminal charges were against Gary, not me, because I'd read the summons. I didn't want to tell Oxford Shoes that, either.

Gary is a speed freak and a smack head. He lies all the time just to make things go his way, and then he denies it, even to himself. I guess he'd lied to Oxford Shoes too and told him I was the one driving.

He'd also said he'd come back to see me when Gary wasn't in. I think Gary left the front door unlocked on purpose that morning so Oxford Shoes could walk right on inside but was prevented by the junk mail and me stamping on his foot. I wasn't about to be anyone's payment for a debt. No Class A drug here.

"Here's your fucking car. Now fucking HAVE IT!" I got the car keys out of my pocket, and I threw them across the street. I was passed the point of no return. I stormed off, leaving the car behind. I couldn't be doing with that car anymore. It wasn't worth the risk. I left him standing there, speechless with his mouth wide open. I wasn't going to be an object in their business, so I gave him the car, along with the attached criminal offences.

I went to the phone box and rang for a cab to pick me up from the house in half an hour. I hurried back to the house, ran upstairs, and as expected Gary wasn't there now. I felt out of breath and overwhelmed by reality, so I searched the room for that wrap from last night. I lifted up the mattress, and there it was. I opened it, and there was nothing left.

Defeated and scared, I packed my things quickly by stuffing my clothes into a few bags, unplugged my stereo and speakers, and gathered my CD's.

I went into the kitchen and opened the drawer where I'd shoved his letters, including the court summons to attend the hearing for his alleged road traffic and drug related offences. I grabbed the letters and lighter. I took them into the back garden, and I used the lighter to set fire to all his letters. I let his junk mail fall on the grass, and I watched it burn. *Gary won't be able to read those now. He'll get time for all the shit he's done.*

I can leave. He won't be able to come after me if he's inside.

It's either him that does the time or me. It's my life. It's mine to change.

I had to make a choice. I waited for my cab.

A Letter from Bangladesh
By Jasmine Jaim

November 24, 2016
Dhaka, Bangladesh

Dear Nabila,

Thanks for your letter! Nice to know that you've found my interview valuable for your research. Nevertheless, while undertaking my interview, it seemed to me that your interest was not limited to the research concerning small businesses of the Bangladeshi women. While conducting the study, you were also passionately exploring your country of origin. As you mentioned earlier, you were born and brought up in England but always had an emotional attachment with Bangladesh. That's why, for your personal interest, I don't mind disclosing some of the issues in this letter.

I think I've got your question right. In the letter, you've asked why I mentioned my children's education several times during the interview. Apparently, this issue was not relevant to your questions regarding the business. Though in fact, I always feel that there exists an intertwined relationship of my business and my personal life. However, while responding to your specific enquiry, interestingly, I have revealed this relationship in a different manner.

In society, we, who are engaged in jobs or businesses,

are often accused of not properly performing our roles as mothers. But for me, I realised how my role as a mother has been constructively shaped by my experiences of the livelihood. Let me tell you that story.

Around forty years ago, I got married to an educated, handsome guy. I was only nineteen years old, and he was in his mid-twenties. The marriage was arranged by my father. I didn't meet him before the wedding and didn't have much to say about the issue. Sounds strange to you? In fact, during that period, in that socio-cultural setting, my approach concerning the marriage was "normal." However, considering the young chap's personality, professional life, family background, and other issues, apparently, it was a good decision of my father's.

After the wedding, I got to know my husband, and within a few months, I realised he was not the right person for me. One morning, when I was leaving for my college, my husband stopped me.

"You don't have to study now. You are already married. Concentrate on your household work."

His comments implied that as long as a woman doesn't get married, she may continue studying. But after getting married, her only focus should be the family life. Seemingly, there is no point to study for a career. Unfortunately, during that period, this scenario was applicable for most of the middle class women in our society. So, I couldn't argue much and had to accept his decision. I tried to confine myself to the marital and maternal roles.

Nonetheless, I faced a different type of difficulty in my conjugal life; one that isn't common for women who attempted to become happy with the only identity of "housewife." That handsome guy I married loved to lead a luxurious life. He spent almost the entire salary on himself.

My children and I had to rely on my father-in-law's earnings from the property and sometimes, even, from my father's money as well. At a certain point, my husband left his job and went to Italy to seek a better living standard. Not surprisingly, rather than sending money to us, he asked for money from his father to maintain his expenditures while living away from us. My father-in-law needed to sell a part of his property to raise more money. Finally, after two years, when my husband returned home, we were in hardship. You might be shocked to know that my husband declared he no longer wanted to work at any job. On top of that, his way of spending remained the same. Literally, I couldn't find any way to maintain the family income, particularly whilst we had three kids and several in-laws living at the same house!

When I felt completely helpless, my father took my children and me to his house. My husband came several times to take us back home. Initially, I couldn't consider going back to that life. You might pose a question—why didn't I think about divorce? It's tough to explain the issue in this letter. The only thing I can say is this: in our society, that was the period when we didn't want to think about divorce as an option.

Finally, after staying for nearly two years at my father's house, I decided to go back. At the age of nineteen, when I went to my husband's house for the first time, that was my father's decision, but, this time, when I returned to that house with my kids, it was my decision. I'd like to add that it was a rational decision. I was concerned what would happen when my father died. My elder brother assured me that, in the absence of my father, he would support me financially. However, I realised that in the long run, he might struggle to maintain the expenditure of my family. Moreover, in our society, it's a shame for a married woman to depend on the money of the natal family. The situation compelled me to consider a way to earn my own income.

When I went back to my house, I had to play a different role. At the initial stage of my family life, I had to follow my husband's orders by engaging myself in only "household chores," but now, I needed to position myself in the family to go beyond that boundary. As I did not complete the undergraduate program, I wasn't eligible to apply for any decent job. Even though, because of my husband, I was desperate to earn, it was he who set the major obstacle (my lack of education) for earnings. So sad! However, apparently, the only way forward was to develop a business. I was good at preparing handicraft products and hence, decided to produce boutique products.

Again, my husband could not accept the issue easily.

He said rigidly, "A business is not for a woman. Stop doing so."

I said, "Leave the issue—whether it is for a woman or not. Personally, I don't enjoy forming a business. But how will we survive?"

He ignored the question, but firmly said, "You can't go into business."

We had arguments so many times, but he never came up with a rational solution regarding the earnings for the family. I could not pay attention to his opinions, though perhaps, "orders" is a better word. The necessity of supporting my family led me to continue my work, regardless of his negative attitude.

Honestly, I didn't enjoy the work of doing the business. Although I had emotional support from my father and elder brother, practically no one helped me in my business. I had to complete my domestic works and then had to work for my business. It was really very tough for me to manage all these different kinds of work together. It was very challenging, particularly, because my investment was so small. Initially, I could not have many employees or many machines. I had to find out the way to develop and carry on my business with extremely limited financial capital. There were many sleepless nights when I needed to work to meet the deadline of the orders. It was really hard to work in that manner. I took several years to establish my business. And, considering my effort and time, I earned far less money than I wanted to.

I knew that if I were in a regular job, I could earn more money. Compared to my small business, I wouldn't have to work so hard in a job, but I could earn a handsome amount of money to maintain my family. In fact, if I could have a job, I would not face such problems at the early stage of my family life. I wouldn't feel so helpless and wouldn't need to depend on my father or brother. My family wouldn't be in such an uncertain position. Proper education is a very important issue—I have learned that the hard way.

Due to my experiences, I was determined to educate my children. I was so concerned about the matter that I decided not to arrange marriage of my daughters before their completion of their masters' degrees. I didn't want to leave the issue of education to the "good will" of their husbands. Two daughters got married after post-graduation. The youngest one has fallen in love with someone. Still, she is waiting for her wedding because she is continuing her studies. As my children witnessed my sufferings, all my daughters willingly accepted my decision regarding their marriages. Their father did not interfere in this matter. In fact, he was never much involved in our children's upbringing.

I feel proud that all my children are properly educated.

My eldest daughter is a mid-level manager in a bank. My second daughter is a lecturer in a college. I have only one son. He is also a manager in a bank. All three of them have completed their masters' degree before seeking a job. My youngest daughter is now continuing her masters' degree in micro-biology in a reputed university of the country. I consider educating all my children as the greatest achievement in my life. All my children can earn by themselves. They will not struggle the way I did.

Due to my devotion for the family, I didn't give up in an adverse situation; I tried to find a way, perhaps a very hard way, to overcome my drawback concerning education in order to maintain my family. Nonetheless, my life experiences didn't simply teach me to figure out ways to go forward with determination in the unfavourable situation. Rather, I tried to identify my limitation and develop my children so that they would not need to take such a hard way. I transmitted the learnings from my experiences to my daughters, my next generation, with the hope that the story of struggle will not be repeated.

With warm wishes,

Amira Sultana

MOVING ON
By Becky

It was a normal school day in July 2011, nearing the end of term. My mum picked me and my brother up from school and took us to a pub. It was there she met a bloke who didn't look like a very promising man to know. He had badly done tattoos everywhere, all over his neck and arms. He looked a bit like an alcoholic, was scruffy, and had bad teeth. They were yellow, crooked, and some of them were missing. I ignored all that and thought that because he might really care for my mum, I'd give him a chance. I was only ten at the time, and there were lots of people around me who looked like that, and I hadn't had any bad experiences until then. We stayed at the pub for a couple of hours, getting to know him, and he actually seemed okay.

We were living with my gran in Nottingham at the time because mum had just split with her previous partner. The travelling was quite hard for us, as my mum couldn't keep travelling from Nottingham to Kirkby every morning (for school and work), so she decided it was best for us to move a lot closer to our hometown, which is Kirkby. We moved into a new house in Sutton on the 3rd October with her new partner, the guy from the pub, and we settled in quite quickly. It was so much easier for my brother and I, as we were much closer to school and work. It also meant that I could start a routine where I'd go to my dad's for a whole week and then go back to my mum's for a week. I really liked that, because when we were in Nottingham, I'd hardly seen him.

Everything was going fine until New Year's Eve, when my mum's partner told one of his daughters, who didn't live with us, that he was going to leave my mum to live with a woman he knew. His daughter had become one of my mum's friends, so she told my mum. My brother and I were staying at my dad's house at the time, and she rang my brother to tell him what had happened. She seemed really upset, and I think she was crying because she was struggling to speak. My dad was fed up with the whole situation. He was worried about his kids, and he threatened to kill Mum's boyfriend if he ever hurt us.

I went back home to mum to check on her and give her support, Mr. X moved out two days later. I always wanted to go back to her place when I was at my dad's, even though I enjoyed being there, because I felt the need to protect her. It only took a few days before he came back around, asking Mum to take him back, and apologising for what he'd done. It wasn't long before Mum let him come home permanently. It annoyed me, because I didn't want her to give him another chance. He should never have left in the first place, and I didn't trust him anymore. I hated that he'd hurt my mum.

Soon, everything began to go downhill. He'd leave for a few days and stay at some other woman's house or with his mates. This happened three or four times in just a few months. He spent a lot of time with his mates, smoking weed and drinking alcohol, and kept coming home drunk. When he got home, he'd kick off, smashing car windows, and would argue with my mum. He had a go at me and my brother about a photograph of he and my mum together he'd found in the back of the fireplace. It must've slipped down the gap at the back of it, but he was convinced one of us had dropped it there. In the end, he tore it up and threw it away. That was the first time he really had a go at us. The only other time was when I refused to get in a car with him because he didn't have a license, but he just shouted at me.

Most of the time, my brother would simply remove himself from the situation. He'd go out or stay in his room. He was protective in some ways. When there was a lot of arguing, he'd come into my room to check. Although it was nice that he did that, there wasn't anything that could really help because it was so bad. He's really protective now, and I think we're even closer now because of all we've gone through.

On 1st June, 2012, it was my mum's birthday and he kicked off. He broke his computer chair, picked up my mum's laptop, and slammed it onto the hard floor, smashing it. He punched the wall and door and left a big dint in the door. Mum told me he'd thrown a glass beer bottle at her but fortunately, it had just missed her head. I was upstairs and was petrified by all the noise. I was starting to get really scared. I didn't know how my brother was handling it because he doesn't really show his feelings, and he still doesn't talk about it. My mum was a mixture of stressed, annoyed, and upset. And because she wouldn't do anything about him, I started to get more annoyed with my mum, too. I didn't like living in a house that was so chaotic all the time.

In July, I left primary school and wanted to go to Kirkby College even though there was a school closer to the house. It was where all my friends were going, and it was familiar territory. He argued about what school I should've gone to and tried to force me to walk to my new secondary school, instead of mum driving me there. He wanted control over everything. Luckily, Mum ignored his protests, and I got to go to the school I wanted to go to. Later that year, he and my mum had another argument. My mum told me that the kettle had just boiled, and he picked it up to throw it at her, but it all poured down his arm. He dropped it and got my mum by the neck and had thrown her against the glass table in the kitchen. He ended up with third degree burns. I was at school at the time, and although being at school meant I was safe and away from the terror of being at home, I also wanted to be at home to protect her. I wasn't there that day, and I'm still not sure how I feel about it. I didn't find out about that fight until about four years later, when I started to write this story, and she started to fill in some gaps. Throughout the year, he kept leaving my mum and coming back home a few days or a week later. I kept saying that she didn't need him and that he wasn't someone to be with. She kept saying he was fine and okay, and that she loved him. I didn't care. He just shouldn't be doing this.

Around September 2013, my mum had finally given up with him. She'd become friends with his ex-wife, and I think she'd finally convinced Mum to get out of the situation. I think she was also worried about us and the effect the relationship was having on us. She went out to find a house while he went out with his mates. While he was out, my mum started to move out a little bit at a time so he wouldn't notice. This was happening when I was in school, but my brother had already left school so he was helping mum move everything. It took days for us to move our stuff because we had to keep waiting for him to go out through the week and the weekend. It took about a week, but we finally moved everything out and made the move to the new house...we were finally able to leave him behind. The first night we stopped in the new house, my mum was getting messages from him, telling her how very sorry he was and that he could sort himself out for her. He'd gone back to the house to find it empty; she'd finally left him, and this time, it was real.

About a month later, I was on my way back from school, and I messaged Mum to tell her that I was coming home with my friend to show her the new house. She didn't respond, but I didn't think anything of it. We walked in on him attacking my mum viciously, but he stopped as soon as we walked in. He turned to me and asked if I wanted them to be together. My mum was behind him miming what I should say. I said, "No, I really don't want you together. Just leave her alone and get on with your own life." He took my mum's purse and walked out. I told my mum to ring the police, but she didn't. She rang someone else instead, but I don't know who. Whoever it was, they didn't come to help. My friend and I went to her house where it was a lot calmer. I was confused about how he found us, and I was worried about my mum.

Later that night, my mum started to get threatening messages from him, telling her that he was going to burn the house down while we were all asleep. Finally, because her kids were in danger, Mum rang the police, and they came around to the house. She printed out all the messages and showed them, and she told them about all the other things he'd done to her over the past couple of years. She filed an official report. Fortunately, Mum didn't have any serious injuries, just bruises.

He went to Spain for two weeks to escape from the police, because they were trying to arrest him. But the UK police contacted the Spanish police and because of extradition laws, he was sent back. When he came home, he handed himself into the police, and they arrested him. The police were involved, and he was sent to court. He pleaded guilty and was sent to prison. She must have protected me from it, as I hardly remember any of it.

After that, he's not bothered with her again. Thankfully, to this day, I've not seen him.

Now, my mum has found a much better person. He used to be an alcoholic until he found out he had liver damage, but he's never been anything but caring with her. I've now moved on, and I'm happier. It hasn't affected my relationships, because I know the difference between right and wrong, and I've chosen to be with someone who is very gentle and kind.

It's scary being a child in a domestic violence situation. If someone told me they were going through what I went through, I'd tell them not to hide. Tell people what's going on so they can help you. Nothing that's happening is your fault. And, once you're out, never look back on the past. Concentrate on what is coming towards you in the future. Don't let the past put you down. The future is what you make it.

FRIDAY ROSES
By Cath Bore

The red roses Brian sends on Fridays are delivered to the house, bound in a tight bundle. The taut rubber band pinks my fingers, and thorny stems long and tentacular splice my skin as I unpick the stubborn brown rubber. My fingers cut and bleed but I push the flowers into a vase.

"Have they arrived, the flowers?" Brian rings up and asks, as always. Right on cue. He can't wait. It's too urgent. He needs to know.

"Yes, they've arrived."

Silence.

"Thank you." I wait for the next question. My answer is ready. I have the words, right here.

"And do you like them?" He asks this each time too.

"I love them."

He makes me say it every week. Forces me to lie. Three words. Three syllables. And I squeeze them out on cue. I love them. I love you.

I'm a liar. Sometimes I think he knows that I hate the roses more than I despise him. They offer up no scent, no consolation. The sharp petals scratch the end of my nose as he forces me to sniff them and inhale plain air that smells of tap water.

"Flowers every week. How romantic," everyone says. "You're so lucky."

"Yes." I smile. "I'm lucky."

My cracked ribs creak as I force uncomfortable words out from lips stiff and awkward with lies.

In the end, all it takes is a little push. I watch Brian fall down the stairs, arms in frantic circles, hands grabbing air, and gob flapping silently. He can't believe my audacity. Nor can I. I haven't fought back, ever. Until now. Foul words are snatched from his mouth, air frozen in his lungs. I taste copper in my mouth and smell its perfume. I realise I've bitten my tongue, and I hold it between my teeth as he windmills downwards, legs pedalling.

He hits the ground.

He breaks.

Is still.

Relief washes through me like a flood, and the police believe my tears. They're embarrassed during the interview, apologise for all the questions.

"Red tape, you know?"

I nod that it's okay. Because it is okay. Everything is okay now.

The following Friday, my roses arrive as usual.

Red like blood.

FERN BANK
By Rosie Jarrett

Susanna peered through the windows of the old cottage.
She couldn't see much because dirty net curtains obscured
her view. All she could make out was some sort of arm
chair and piles of boxes. The place didn't look inhabited,
but best be sure. She forced her way to the front door,
scratching her bare legs on the brambles that had invaded
the path. Susanna was confronted by peeling blue paint and
a small metal sign that said "Fern Bank." She felt a shiver of
excitement run through her. What a romantic name, much
better than "10 Fosters Way." She knocked on the door
timidly, thinking up a story in case someone answered. No
sound came from inside. Then she plucked up the courage
to knock harder, and a pane shifted in the little stained glass
window above her head. *Oh dear! I don't want to damage
anything.* Susanna had learnt about squatting from her
mate, Andy, and knew that you had to be careful with the
property. Weighing things up, she decided that it was far
better than her present accommodation with a cocaine
addict for a partner, an extremely aggressive dog, and a
constant stream of troublesome visitors.

Next Susanna tried the side gate. It was locked, so she
shimmied up the wall and leant over to see what was
holding it. Just a rusty bolt, no problem, but after a few
pulls, she realised that it wasn't going to shift. Suddenly, she

heard footsteps from the street and jumped back down. It was an elderly gentleman, who gave her a wave.

"Glad to see someone's taking an interest in the old place. It's been such a mess since Mrs Frobisher died."

"Oh yes, I know what you mean," Susanna replied. "I'm her great niece. I'm just checking on things for the family."

She breathed a sigh of relief as the old man smiled and said, "Well I mustn't keep you from your duties." And he walked on down the street.

Years of covering for Ray, her drug-drenched partner, had honed her ability to lie and steal. In fact, she'd been responsible for one or two incidents of stealing by stealth, but she had paid her dues by doing community service and no longer squirmed in her sleep at night. Anyway, she needed to get into the house before someone else walked by, so she threw her bag over the gate and jumped after it, landing in a patch of nettles. She held her breath until the pain subsided.

The long, narrow garden was chock-a-block with bushes, weeds, and to her delight, trees. It was summer, and she could see that one or two were covered in apples and maybe plums. However, it was more important to get the back door open than to stare at the yard. She picked up her holdall and dropped it on the nettles in front of her, then kicked it forward slowly. Brambles were harder. There was one large one between her and the door. In the end, she took out the kitchen knife that she'd brought from home and hacked it down. She tossed the bramble to one side and worked her way carefully toward the wooden door. It was firmly locked, but the window next to it was a mess; bits of glass held together with sticky plastic. She pushed at it, and the whole thing caved in. Fortunately she was skinny, as this was a small cottage with small windows. She squeezed through the opening and stumbled away from the glass on the floor. Then she threw her bag down and sat on it. Sweat was running down her face, and the scratches on her legs from the brambles and nettle stings began to hurt. Suddenly she was crying and shaking. Anything was better than last night, which she had felt was going to be her last. Ray had wanted his mates to stay over, and she hadn't. She just wanted to sleep and recover from the weekend when she'd got a bit pissed up. He'd become relentless, chucking her dinner on the floor, and banging on the bedroom door when she'd gone up there for some peace. Even when she'd given in and said they could come, he'd swore at her and called her a mean bitch for not joining in. In the end, she'd locked herself in the bathroom and hatched a plan. She'd left at dawn and spent all day wandering the streets of their small town, trying to find somewhere empty and secluded to squat.

Susanna looked up. The sunlight from the dirty window illuminated a painting on the side wall. She peered at a woman in a dark dress with her hair in some sort of bun. She didn't look unpleasant, more vacant, as though she was wishing for better things. Susanna felt sympathy for the woman and decided to clean the painting up when she had the time. Finding the best room to sleep in wasn't a problem, as the front room was full of rubbish, and the stairs looked decidedly dodgy. So, she stuck to the room at the back with the picture in it. There was a little stone floored scullery to one side with a sink and cupboards. The taps didn't work, but she could sort that out in the morning. There was a brush in one corner which she used to clean her sleeping area. Then she took out her sleeping bag and laid it carefully below the window. She was a bit bothered by the lack of glass. It didn't make her feel safe, so she found some old bits of board to wedge into it. Exhausted, she lay down and drifted off to sleep. She woke a couple of hours later desperate for a wee. It wasn't quite dark, so she removed the boards and squeezed herself out of the window and into the garden. A bat fluttered by, and she shivered in excitement. No Ray, no bills, and a real animal in a real garden with bushes and trees, not piles of junk. Back inside, Susanna set about preparing the food that she'd brought with her. It was a bit complicated because she had cutlery but no plate. She had baked beans and a tin opener, but nothing to heat them with.

"You'll find a plate in the cupboard next to the sink."

Susanna started and looked around. There was no one there. It wasn't a frightening voice, so she decided to follow the advice. Sure enough, there was a pile of old white plates in the cupboard along with bowls and glasses. They looked quite clean, so she decided to risk it and rinsed a plate and glass with the bottled water she'd brought. She didn't get any advice on cooking, so settled for cold beans, bread, and a piece of cheese, and washed it down with rum and coke. She'd been saving the rum for her birthday in three weeks' time. *What the heck. This is my birthday. New me, new life.* She poured herself another.

***

Susanna woke the next morning refreshed but in need of a wash. She went to the scullery and started searching for the stop tap.

"You have to turn the water on outside, dear." It was the voice again.

Susanna plucked up the courage to respond, even though she felt stupid.

"Where can I do that?"

"There's a little square cover outside the back door. You might need a tool. My father always kept one in the shed."

Susanna's consternation was outweighed by her need for a wash and the feeling that she'd rather live with a ghost than Ray any day. He was useless at practical things; she was always the one changing light bulbs and replacing broken windows. She knocked open the bolts on the back door then noticed a key hanging on the wall. It worked. Next, she cleared the weeds outside with the kitchen knife and discovered a small metal cover. Getting into the shed was a nightmare, but after half an hour of pulling and chopping a massive creeper, she was standing looking at a real work bench with rows of tools hanging above it.

The voice spoke again. "My father spent hours in here. He made me a toy horse once. I think it's still in the attic."

"Oh," said Susanna. "My father never did much at home except watch TV and moan at my mum because we were making too much noise." Susannah found it difficult enough talking to strangers, let alone a ghost. Still, she kept talking.

"Poor dear!" the voice replied. "Anyway, I'm sure this is the one."

A long metal bar with a bulge on the end started moving from side to side. Susanna started then carefully reached for the tool. She felt something brush her hand as she took it off the hook. A few yanks, and the stopcock opened. She rushed to the sink. The water came out rusty brown at first but then cleared. She threw off her clothes, climbed into the large sink, and bathed.

"Really, dear, what if the neighbours see?"

Susanna laughed and threw water into the corner where the voice was coming from. She had the rest of the day to herself and spent it washing, tidying, and sweeping.

The front room was full of old magazines and books. She sorted them into piles according to what she thought they were worth. Her mind kept wandering back to Ray and his insistence on her taking things to be pawned and sold. She knew the ropes, but he might be looking for her, and she couldn't risk taking them to any local dealer.

"If only I had a friend in this time of crisis!" Susanna said.

"I'm your friend. Just don't throw water at me," said the voice.

"Okay, truce," said Susanna. "But you have to start by telling me your name and who you are."

The ghost was evasive. "Well, you've seen me, you know, and this was my house before Mr and Mrs Frobisher got their hands on it."

Susanna remembered the woman in the black dress.

"Do you wear your hair in a bun?" she asked.

"That's me, dear."

"Your name?" Susanna asked gently. She'd noticed a disturbed tone in the woman's voice.

"Emily Taylor."

Emily seemed to find talking about herself difficult. "Well, thank you for being my friend," she said, "perhaps we can talk more tomorrow?"

"Yes, yes, I have to prepare my father's supper now. He doesn't like to be kept waiting."

Susanna heard a noise in the scullery and decided to stay put until Emily had finished.

***

The next day Susanna felt a hand shake her awake.

"Look, dear, I can only spare you half an hour, but there's something in the attic that might interest you."

Susanna could see the outline of a figure standing over her. It was Emily. She pulled on some jeans and a shirt and headed for the stairs. Clinging to the bannister, she edged her way up to the first floor.

"This way, dear," Emily said.

She entered a small bedroom with a sloping ceiling. A panel at one side began to move, slowly revealing a wooden horse, and a large tin trunk. The lock on the trunk rattled, and the lid swung open.

"These might be of some use to you. I've no more need of them now." Emily seemed more focussed.

Susanna peered into the trunk. It was full of clothes, properly retro. She wanted to hug Emily, but instead she felt a hand in hers.

"You've been a good help to me, tidying up the house, Susanna, and I think you'd better look after Fern Bank now. I've realised that my father is dead, and my mother has been calling me from the other side for a long time."

Susanna felt a huge wave of relief sweep over her. Maybe she could invite some of her living friends around now. Sharing Fern Bank with Emily and all her interruptions and surprises hadn't been easy, but it had certainly been worth it. Her new life was calling.

TRUTH OR FICTION
By Morag Campbell

There's a big box of Rose's chocolates on my lap, the kind
you get at Christmas. And I'm lying in a huge, crumpled,
messy bed. Someone has given me these chocolates, though
I can't remember who. The room is dark. But there is a light.
Not from the window, though. If I turn my head to the right,
I can see a lamp, like a crystal. There's a glow surrounding
the crystal. I don't know where I am. This is a dream. It must
be. I try to wake up. But everything stays the same. I look
at the chocolates. Coffee flavour is my favourite, but right
now I don't want chocolate. I'm wearing a vest but nothing
else. I feel naked and cold, and I look for my clothes. I can't
see them anywhere. There are some ladies' dresses in a
wardrobe on the other side of the room. I pull out a blue
silky satin one. It smells of sweat and Pond's cold cream. It
doesn't look clean, and I can see flecks of pink face powder.
It's too big for me. Still, I wrap the petticoat around me.
There's a big dressing table with pots of makeup, and against
it I can see a screen with three lacy bras hanging over it.
Behind the long velvet curtains I can see daylight beginning
to show through. I'm not breathing. I'm scared. I know that
someone will be coming back, but I don't remember who it
is.

My head is fuzzy, and I feel sick. My tongue feels thick
in my mouth. I think I've been sick, thrown up somewhere.

There's a brown stain on my vest. I need to wee, but I can't go out without my clothes. In the corner there's a doorway. I pull hard on the handle, but it's stuck and nothing moves. I pull again with all my strength, and it opens. It's a cupboard with shelves full of sheets and towels. I hear voices. Loud, like the men shouting as they fall out of the pub on a Friday night. I crouch at the bottom of the cupboard and close the door. It's dark inside, but I pull the laundry bag on top of me.

"Hide and seek time!"

Someone is opening the door of the wardrobe. "Try under the bed."

It's my Uncle Joe, just back from the army. Brought us all presents from Aden, a long way away.

"Naw, she's no' there. Try the cupboard."

I move further back, covering myself with a loose board.

"Nuh."

"The wee brat, she's disappeared. The door was locked. How did she get oot?" Joe again.

"Ah paid you good money for hur. Let's see it back an' am oot ah here. You're asking fur trouble wi hur on the loose. You said she wid do whit she wis telt."

"She's git a hauf bottle o' Whyte and Mackays inside 'er. She wis comatose. She's no gone far. Ye need tae help me find 'er, or ahm toast. Margaret'll kill me."

"Ah've had enuff. Whaur's ma munney? This is nae ma fault. You talked me intae it. Said nuthin' could gae wrong. Well, it's wrang noo. Helluva wrong. Money, noo!"

"Ye'll need tae wait. Whit do ye think bought the Whyte and Mackays and a nice double room fae the night?"

"Yoo got this fur a favour, nae questions asked. Have ah got tae turn yoo upside doon and shake y'ur bliddy brains oot afore ah git ma money?"

Sounds like Joe counting out the money. I wonder if I

should come out. He's going to find me, and I need the toilet. I'm bursting. I try to pee just a little bit, just to let it out, but it streams out everywhere. They'll hear me. I try to keep it in, but it's no use. It's too late. I wrap a towel around me and push the wet petticoat into the corner. I start to cry. I try to stop and start to hiccup. The room is quiet. They must have gone. Now the sobs come, and I can't stop them.

The door opens. It's Uncle Joe.

"Ya wee bitch, ah knew you were still in here somewhere. Oot, oot! Whit's that smell? Whit's that puddle? Ya fuckin' wee bitch, wis that you? You're too big tae go wettin' yersel'. Whit're ye doin' in the cupboard? Ur ye mad, that's no' a toilet. Whit ur yae doin' in there? An' noo ahve lost a gid customer. You cost me money. That wis ah a gid thing that ah hud goin'. Ah telt ye, didn't ah tell ye? Ye said ye wid do whit ye wir telt." He looks around, searching. "Whaur's that half croon ah gave ye? Ye've lost it! Ya durty wee tramp, look at the state o' ye!"

He's grabbing my hair and pulling me out. I trip up, and the towel falls off.

"Ya durty wee tramp, look at ye!"

I twist to avoid his fist and trip on the towel wrapped around my feet. He picks me up and throws me across the room. My head hits the wall, and I...

***

I pause. How to finish this gruesome story emerging from my pen?

"Two minutes to finish." The tutor looks around, smiles, then carries on typing her own story onto her laptop.

My concentration has gone. I stop. I don't want to think about what happens next. I'm confused. Is this a memory?

Or simply a story arising from our guided visualisation exercise? But the voices are strong. The uncle is real. And yes, I know he was a nasty piece of work, more than capable of doing something like this.

I read my story to the class, emphasising the broad Glaswegian accent of my childhood. I thought I'd lost my accent, but the strong rich syllables roll off my tongue like it all happened yesterday. The teacher likes it and tells me I must read my work in public. I'm pleased and flattered, but can't imagine anyone can find it entertaining. Perhaps I'll take a class, memoir.

Yes, that sounds good. Writing for wellbeing. Complex PTSD, dissociation, depression. I thought it was all behind me. My life is good. I travel. I have friends and a good business. The nightmares have gone, at least when I'm asleep. My teacher wants me to write a novel.

Real life in fiction. Perhaps I'll go somewhere warm, find a writing community, a villa with pool near the sea where I can rewrite the memories into oblivion, or perhaps into a bestseller. Who knows?

Moments Upon Moments
By Shane

What're the most important points in your life? These are just a few of mine.

2nd March 2016 (the most important one so far)
I realised that there was a point in living. I can say that on 2nd March, I was the happiest person alive.

15 June 2015
I finally told my mum about what my cousin had done to me. What does this have to do with my situation? How did two vital points in my life come about, and how are they linked to my story?

It all started when my mum and dad split in 2003; I was three, and my brother, Connor was two, Daniel was five, Michael was seven, and my younger sister, Alicia, was only a couple of months old. A year after they'd split up, my mum had many partners, but eventually found "the right one for her," and she's been with him ever since. During this time, for reasons I don't want to go into here, there were lots of court visits and social workers coming in and out of our lives.

There came a time when I became frightened to go to my mums' friend's house, who lived across the road from us. I'd started to kick off as I no longer liked going there. My mum thought I was kicking off for the sake of it, but I dreaded going as I knew I'd have to do it again. Her friend's son, Keith, was a lot older than me.

He used to ask, "Do you want to play a game?"

I would reply, "But it hurts."

He'd say, "It won't, it's a different game this time." He'd get angry if I said no, so I did what he wanted me to. When I was four, he said to me, "You don't need to tell your mum or dad, as it's our secret game."

So I didn't tell anyone, and I did what he told me to do, until he did it more and more, and I couldn't handle it any longer. I'd cry when getting sent to bed when we stayed at Dawn's house. I knew he'd take me into his room and say we're going to play *Row the boat*, but when we played it at school, I wasn't playing it like this. It was different and it didn't hurt me, whereas this one did. But when I said this isn't the normal game that we play at school, he'd laugh.

"No, it's a more secret game of row the boat."

I said no more about it, until one Tuesday when I was five years old, when my mum was at the chippy. We always had a chip cob for our tea on Tuesdays. I was at home with my step dad, who was on the computer like he always was. I turned and asked him a really strange question for someone of my age (again, sorry, but I'm not ready to tell you what the question was).

He said, "Pardon, sweet heart, I didn't quite hear what you said."

I said, "It doesn't matter."

Whether he heard me and was that shocked he wanted me to repeat it, or whether he genuinely didn't hear me, I don't know. But he insisted that I asked him again, so I did.

His response was, "How do you even know about that?"

I told him what had happened at Dawn's house. My step dad sat me down and asked who the person was. When I told him who it was, I can remember him looking very stern.

He said, "It's okay, Chrissy, we're going to sort this out.

You've done so well to tell me. Well done."

My mum arrived back from the chip shop, and my step dad asked me to stay in the room, but asked my older brother to take everyone else up the stairs. I told my mum and step dad everything. All I can remember was that my mum flooded up with tears, and I hugged her and said, "It's okay. Dad's going to sort it out."

From that day onwards, I remember my mum often kept me close by her side. I also remember that we stopped going to Dawn's house. I remember the social worker turned around and said to my mum that we weren't under any circumstance to go there anymore, and I felt so insanely relieved. My mum and stepdad had to take me and my brothers to the police station. We were taken into a room where they asked us questions and taped us. I remember through it all that all I wanted was to see my mama and for her to bring my Ted. It turned out that it wasn't just me he'd been doing it to; he'd done the same thing with my two older brothers and my younger sister. They couldn't figure out if he'd done the same with my younger sister and new born brother, but I remember my mum being distraught about it.

Later, Keith pled not guilty but was found guilty of rape of both my older brothers, my younger brother, and me.

You might be thinking that's enough for one child, and that should be the end of it. So did I.

June 2006

But then, my step dad's twenty-year-old nephew, Steve, (my cousin) came and moved in with us in 2006, when I was six years old. I thought nothing of it until he came into the bedroom one night and started to touch me in inappropriate ways. I told him to stop, but he didn't. I felt trapped, and I didn't know what to do. I tried to shout for my mum because I was panicking. He covered my mouth and whispered that if I told a soul he would sit me on a chair, tie me there, and leave me to die. That kept me quiet for a long time.

I remember crying before coming home after football club, thinking, "How can this be?" I just hoped every day that it was all a nightmare, and I'd wake up from it and never look back again. But I knew it was reality. I thought, "What have I done for this to happen to me again and again?" I would often go out in the rain and burst into tears. I did this because rain is lovely and fresh: it's like Mother Nature is washing you from your worries and telling you, "It's okay to cry. No one can tell whether it's tears on your face or the fresh downpour that I'm throwing on the Earth." All I wanted to do was get myself out of the situation, yet I couldn't risk my family getting hurt again. So I kept quiet and dreaded going home every night, even though I knew I'd have to go through hell and back, or that's what it seemed like to me. But I knew it was wrong.

Every night I would say that I wanted to tell my mum, but he said he would kill her, my brother, and my mama. I'd build up the courage to tell Mum, but then worry that if I did, she'd be dead by the time I got home. I loved going to school, because I didn't have to face him through the whole day. When I was ill, I wouldn't tell my mum for fear of her making me stay at home. I knew if I was at home, I'd have to put up with the same things as I did at night. If I was ill at school, I wouldn't tell anyone because I didn't want to go home. I knew he'd be there. It seemed that everywhere I went, he was there, and the only place I felt safe was school. I wanted to be there every opportunity I had.

Then, finally, my step dad found Steve a place to live in sheltered accommodation, and he moved out. I thought I was safe again. I was relieved, but lived in the fear he would still return.

I was safe for about six months, until he was kicked out because he wouldn't come in before curfew.

Again, I panicked. I cried at school. Fortunately, he didn't move back in with us. One night, my younger sister went into my mum and stepdad's room and told them about what Steve, my cousin, had done to her too. She was afraid he'd come back to live with us and decided to say something. I had no idea what he had done to her at this point in time. That night, I was asked a number of questions by my mum, but because of what Steve said he would do if I told anyone, I wouldn't tell my mum the truth. I just denied everything she asked me about. It was then that my mum told me what Alisha had said, but I was scared to tell as I didn't want harm to come to my family. Still, my mum rang the police.

All he got was an order to stay away from children. The police couldn't follow through with a proper investigation because Alisha was unstable and couldn't go through the whole court process.

Every night since that day, I've hated myself for not telling anyone about it earlier, because he could've been sent down.

2nd March 2016

It wasn't until at school when I was doing PSHE that I finally broke down in Miss Dove's classroom. She sent me to Miss Bower's room (she's the safe guarding officer at school), and I told her everything. I was petrified in case Steve followed through with his threats against my mum or the rest of my family.

I have the flashbacks of the night he threatened me. I'd go to bed but have nightmares every night. These caused sleep deprivation and made me feel like I no longer wanted to be here. The abuse over the years had finally gotten on top of me, and although I tried to get hold of CAMHS, they didn't get back to me. I felt like there was no one and nowhere to turn. The internal stuff was more than the support I had. Which is what caused me to no longer want to be here, and I took all my anti-depressants at once hoping to be done with it all. As I went to the lesson, knowing it would soon be over, I got a text message from my partner. It made me reconsider what I was doing and I broke down in tears. I told my teacher what I'd done. I don't remember what the message said, but I know it saved my life.

I was taken to a hospital in an ambulance. I got lumbered with about twenty mental health workers asking me all kinds of questions. They wanted to know if I'd felt like this before, or if I'd do it again. When I got released, I had someone with me everywhere I went. I wasn't allowed to be outside on my own, and I was even escorted to and from school. Family had to take me to my partner's house. My medication was restricted, and somebody had to oversee it.

When I was in the hospital, this person came to me. I don't remember who she was, but she told me that it took her twenty-seven years to come out to her parents. And she said that if she'd been able to become a nurse after what she'd been though, I could become anything I wanted to be as well.

My mom slowly started to trust me to go to places she could find me and know I was safe.

Things started getting better when I came to the realisation that I needed help directly with the abuse, not with other issue. I needed help figuring out how to deal with everything I'd been through. I went back to CAMHS and got the kind of counselling I needed to deal with the flashbacks and such. Then I went to NIDAS to support my partner, and it turns out that was a great decision too.

I know how to sort the flashbacks out now. I have people around me who can help me and a contact number always available. I'm not fully healed yet, but I'm hoping to get there one day. It doesn't matter what someone threatens you with, you must tell someone. If you don't, they'll get away with it. They'll do the same thing they've done to you to others, and that can make you feel like the worst person in the world, the way I did. Reach out. Find support. Don't let them have control.

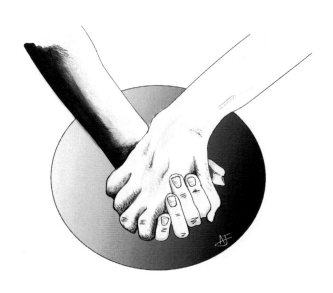

EVER ENDLESS WORDS
By Shane

Many thoughts, yet no consideration,
Just thoughts of unwanted correlation.

Many other sleepless unwanted nights,
When I should be dreaming of flying high kites.

Why, oh why, do I let this happen to myself?
Even though I have the chance to save this soul of mine.

The word came just before the tongue,
About to roll off.

Then the endless threats and promises came flooding back,
With a tear at the bottom of the retina, yet no further the
tear will burst.

The worst of my demons enter my not-so child-like mind,
As my enemies have deprived me of this privilege.

They say keep your friends close and enemies closer, but is
this really the case?
It wasn't in my case. How about yours?

Don't let them beat you down!

YOU MUST KNOW WHAT THEY FEAR
By Kerry Hadley-Pryce

They say a woman's smile is the greatest thing she can possess, but men? Men don't have to have looks. Take Boris Johnson, for example. Daniel Barker is another. What it was about him, I don't know, even now. He had hair, lots of it, red, wiry, and that Boris Johnson-esque sloping face. Not quite perfect, for sure, but still, there was definitely something appealing.

They also say to truly know someone, you must know what they fear. No real gambler, for example, cares about money, and no real drinker gives a shit about health, but in both cases, there's always an element of fear. Daniel Barker was, in the truest sense, a gambler and a drinker. To keep up with him, you had to have nerve. It was poker he played, which is more of a game of chance, except when you introduce the notion of cash, then it gains quite a bit of skill and psychology. Money, to Daniel Parker, meant risk. When he played poker it got risky, and you needed nerve to keep up with him, because he was fast company, and he had no fear about that.

He was, in fact, mad. Crazy. A liar at least half of the time. He operated in a different reality. He was all charm one day and everything seemed possible, and then he'd disappear or ignore you. And that was what gave him power. You were forced to slide into his world, wherever that was, when you were with him. You succumbed to it. He took possession of you.

I said to him once, "How come you're like this, Daniel?"

"Like what, exactly?"

"Don't start that, tell the truth," I said.

"What do you mean?"

And we went on like this, back and forth, pointlessly, until I had to say, "Oh, fuck you, Daniel Barker."

"Hah!" he said eventually. "See. Gotcha."

Once, he told me he'd been married ,but that his wife had committed suicide by jumping off a cliff. The next day, when I asked him about her, he laughed and asked what the hell I was on about. Another time, he told me his mother had locked him in their attic every time he was bad, and then he'd looked at me, all slopey-eyed, and said we should have a child together, that I'd be the only one he'd have a child with.

Several times he disappeared for a few days or a week, and once he hid all my make-up, telling me to go "bare-faced," as I'd look better. When I looked at myself, it was like I was translucent to his brushstroke, like I'd been outwitted.

Another time, he came back tanned and smelling of cigars. Two weeks he'd been away without so much as a word, and he could tell I was angry, but he laughed and offered me a whisky, though he knew I couldn't stand it. When I sulked, he put his arms around my shoulders, told me we were meant to be, and that it was fate.

He called me once at two a.m. I was asleep downstairs. He didn't speak straight away. Eventually, he said he just needed to describe a dream he'd had. He said it made him feel like he'd walked up the wrong staircase, thinking it was the right one, and that he couldn't find the way down again. Something about him tottering and plunging about like you do in the dark, clinging to whatever he could get his hands on, trying to get a grip. He sounded scared. I listened, sympathised, calmed him down.

"You should probably lay off the drink for a bit," I said.

The next day, he sent me flowers with a card that just said, "Sorry. I love you for last night."

Talking to him, though, was like looking into a giant mirror or a gaping abyss, depending on his mood. You felt, literally, like you'd become a two-pair, or maybe not a two-pair. Who knows how you felt. Like climbing a wall is how you felt.

Which is how it all started, really, the climbing.

Six weeks, it was. Six weeks without him. He did one of his disappearing acts. Right after he sent me the flowers. Phone disconnected, emails bounced back. It was like he'd never even existed. My heart hurt. I felt like I'd been stabbed or starved. I thought I'd never, ever, smile again. I started walking the streets at night. Maybe I thought I'd find him hiding somewhere. I can't remember what I was thinking now, but I came across the warmth of the local leisure centre and had accidentally walked into where the climbing wall is. The instructor there thought I'd come for the class. Maybe, deep down, I'd wanted to be there, climbing that wall.

Initially, on my early tries, I got about two feet up. It was ridiculous. I felt like the wall was loose and would tumble back down onto me. I yelped like a small animal. But there were kids there who I watched. I watched them size it up, the wall. I watched them address it like a philosophical proposition. I watched how their fingers worked at it, how their arms and legs tested it, how they had a conversation with it, and then how they pressed themselves on, upwards. How they became *it*. It took me four weeks of practice and perseverance and pain, every night, to climb that wall to the top. I remember that feeling even now. It was like I'd left myself, the person I was, the self I knew, the way I felt about things, at the bottom. I knew nothing would be the same. The kids there gave me high-fives and invited me to a real climb. The Peak District.

Daniel, when he reappeared, looked even more slopey about the face than ever. I could tell he'd been drinking, and I could smell it all over him. It made me feel sick.

"God, look at you," he said. "You're all...sinew. And you're wearing lipstick, I see."

He told me he'd been hunkered down in Birmingham. Digbeth, or somewhere. Said he'd got with an Asian girl, had won her in a poker game, until her family had found out and threatened to cut his throat. Said he'd had to do a runner. I half believed him, but to be honest, I wasn't really listening.

"You're not thinking of going somewhere without me," he said. He'd seen my bags all packed. Not so much a question as a statement of fact.

So, it was basically his idea, but ultimately, I was the one who drove us to the Peak District.

The car filled with his smell. It was as if he'd trodden in something. I had to keep my window open the whole way. He hardly spoke but it didn't bother me. I was above him now, and I knew it. It was like I'd managed to remove a pebble from my shoe.

Hope Valley, when we arrived there, looked like a sleeping giant, and the rock poked up, obscene and ungainly; elephantine. And the valley dipped like a huge, yawning mouth. I felt myself filling up with it, taking on the skin of it, and as I enlarged, I felt him, Daniel, diminishing.

"Look at it," I said. It was an inane thing to say when you look at the words there, but it was more in the way I said it.

Daniel looked at it, the view, then the rock. His eyes were

blue slate. He stretched his neck, and I saw him swallow. He licked his lips, but they stayed dry, and he said something I didn't catch. It was as if the words were sluicing out of him. It felt like he was clinging onto me.

"You're scared," I said. "You really are, aren't you?"

And I wanted to push him at it: the view, the rock, the gambling, the drinking.

He looked at me then. "You're smiling. I haven't seen you smile in, what, months." He was trying to bluff, but I knew then I could possess him. If I wanted to.

Before I'd made the climb, I'd said to Daniel, "I'm leaving the car keys." And I knew he'd felt a shift in footing that he didn't fully understand.

***

From the top of the rock, all there is, is breath and the sight of things more clearly: felled trees lying in gorse; the ditch of a valley with unexpected colour—you wouldn't know the flowers there. There's almost nothing you can do up there, except look. Sometimes small flies bat against your face. You feel your toes and heels burning, your fingertips. There's no phone signal. The road is scorched into the landscape, and you can watch cars disappearing along it, for as long as you like. It makes you smile, it really does.

Which is, after all, the greatest thing a woman can possess.

TAKE NOTICE
By Brey Willows

Helen is an ordinary woman. She lives an ordinary life with an ordinary job. She's not the type of woman to demand a second glance for being either excessively pretty or surpassingly ugly. Most people do not notice Helen.

Helen would, if she had the money, get plastic surgery to make herself look extra-ordinary. But because she has an ordinary job, she has an ordinary paycheck that does not allow for extravagance.

Helen takes an enormous bite of her cheese and peanut butter sandwich and chomps, peeling the sticky mixture from the roof of her mouth with her tongue. She stares out of the fogged-over window of the train, wondering how she can become someone people notice. She is tired of being one of the crowd. She wants heads to turn, even if they don't know her name, Helen Hobowitz. She wants people to want to talk to her because she looks so very extraordinary.

Hefting herself to her feet, she steps off the train and buttons her coat tightly to her neck, absently holding out her hand out to steady the old woman stepping off the train behind her until the woman gives her a semi-grateful nod and shuffles on her way. Walking through the city centre, she hunches against the cold, her scarf creating a sort of hump in the back of her coat. After stooping to pick up a bottle cap for a woman balancing a baby and bags, she continues to duck and dodge and step aside as people pass in a holiday rush.

Helen stops and stares for a moment at a glamorous Calvin Klein ad in a shop window. The woman in the enormous photo is everything Helen is not. She looked tall, elongated, and elegant. Her stomach was flat as a ruler, and she didn't seem to mind the snow flurries fluttering past her tanned bosom. A man passing stumbled as he moved past her, and she grabbed his arm to steady him, acknowledging his mumbled thanks with a slight incline of her head, even as she continued to stare at the woman she wanted to be. Extra-ordinarily pretty. Someone people notice.

With a deep sigh, she pushed her glasses up on the bridge of her nose and stepped into her favourite coffee house. Digging in her enormous floral printed canvas bag, she dropped two cans into the Food for the Homeless box by the door before ordering her skim milk, no foam latte. Dropping two pounds in the tip jar because it's the holidays, she patiently waited for her drink, stepping out of the way, and letting two young women who were clearly in a hurry take the drink meant for her and taking the next one instead.

She climbed the stairs and found her favourite comfy chair occupied. Upset by this unexpected slight to her routine, she went to the other side of the room.

The big comfy chair there, although not nearly as comfortable with not nearly as good a view, is empty, and she sank into it gratefully. She piled the plates and dishes still there together for the server to pick up later, tidied her area, and then sank further into the chair, her hot coffee warming her large, cold hands, and the steam fogging up her glasses.

She gazed out the window while sipping, the last light of day fading as the holiday lights flashed on, their reds and blues highlighting hanging plastic presents high above the street centre. She watched the people below scurrying like ants carrying enormous food packs wrapped in bright bags with casually shouting logos, their faces flushed, their mouths in thin, hard lines as they battled through the masses. They pushed passed one another, their eyes averted, their heads down, immersed in thoughts and worlds of their own. Helen wondered what their lives were like, how interesting they must be to need to rush about so.

As she watched, a woman stumbled past below, laden with a box clearly too heavy for her. Helen grunted when an expensive looking black glove fell from her coat, unnoticed as she struggled through the crowd. A man behind her stepped on it and then dodged passed the woman, nearly knocking her over. Heaving herself up, Helen left her coat and things upstairs, rushed outside, picked up the muddy glove, hurried after the woman, tapped her on the shoulder, showed her the glove with a slight smile, and gently tucked it in the woman's pocket to the sound of the woman's rushed thanks and happy holidays and such.

Back in the coffee house, Helen finished her coffee, gathered her things, buttoned her coat to her neck and walked out into the cold night air, crisp with fresh snow and the sound of carolers over the din of sales clerks ringing up purchase after purchase. She is surrounded by people she would have loved to talk to. To understand what it is that makes them interesting, to know who they are rushing home to, and why.

Standing at the train stop she gently pulled a little boy back by his shoulder as a car raced passed. His mother scolded him and dragged him away. Helen continues to stand there, wondering just what she could do that might make her someone people notice.

THE GREAT SWITCH OFF
By Susan Lapsley

While writing a resolution seems to be a simple task, I'm reminded of all the years where I've failed to keep even one resolution beyond January. This year, however, I intend it to be different and make a real success. I've decided that it should be in the form of an affirmation that I could use every morning prior to the start of my meditation—a practice that is now well and truly established in my life. Affirmations are uplifting and can be powerful statements for change, but they need to be done right. No pressure then! It's important for me to create something meaningful that I can align with, use as a tool to help me stay calm and present during times of stress and anxiety or whatever else that causes me angst. Like now, for example, as I perceive myself procrastinating and doing everything except the very thing I need do.

It's at this time of year, from November onwards, that I'm glued to the television screen every afternoon watching feel-good Christmas movies. I watch them all, every day, and love putting my feet up and soaking in every special feel good moment. However, this somewhat obsessive viewing is not necessarily meant to put me in the festive mood, because mince pies do that all by themselves, it's more to do with avoiding the Christmas hype, and the hordes of shoppers that pour into the streets and the shops, and cram the buses, and trams. This is the kind of nightmare reality that makes me run for the hills, preferring instead to watch people's lives play out on the television screen in all the feel-good movies. In truth, I'm not the kind of person that mixes easily, and I tend to back away from the frenetic rush of life that Christmas brings. I feel almost unhinged amid crowds of people and have to run away, withdraw into the solitude that I love, and my sofa and Christmas movies that beat the standing in long noisy queues hands down. I am very much my own person but recognise I need help with providing the listening ear and gentle support some of my friends appear to need from me at this time.

Looking back, I'd purposely taught myself to withdraw from about the age of thirteen or fourteen onwards. I was confused about everything, and understood nothing of what was going on around me. I knew I had to escape and find a way to cope with it all. What I realised was that nobody appeared to notice that my mind was elsewhere, especially when I was smiling and nodding. But actually, I was far away in a place of my own choosing. I knew even back then that my escape route of going into myself but appearing not to, had worked. I felt empowered by it and expected a future in which I could participate on my own terms. I practised at every opportunity until the day, years later as an adult with more understanding of the world and people, that I began to question the rightness of what I was doing. What if "switching off" was dishonest? What if I was preventing people getting to know the real me? If I was proficiently hiding my true feelings, then how would people know I was telling the truth? How could I be sure that my love for someone was real? Was I really doing people and myself a huge disfavour?

The first time I ignored my escape mechanism or forgot about having such a tool, was one Friday night in early June 1977, when all my energies were so focussed in the present moment that "switching off" was some distant memory. However, I remember feeling like a rose bud suddenly knowing how to open and stretch out its delicately perfumed petals and present them to the waiting world. I'd walked into a busy wine bar on the King's Road in Chelsea, near where I lived, to wait for my flatmate, Pauline. It was buzzing, but fortunately there was an empty seat close to the door that I knew Pauline would like. Opposite me sat a man dressed completely in black with a huge black cape draped casually around his shoulders. He wore a large, black, wide-brimmed hat that covered his long wavy black hair and emphasised a thick bushy black beard. I was intrigued and completely captivated by him, and I was grateful he was so focussed on the entertainment—another attractively handsome man with a beard and hat who was playing a twelve string acoustic guitar and harmonising with a stunningly beautiful female singer at his side. A Fleetwood Mac number, as I recall. Just what had I walked into? A dream, obviously!

I was so lost in my thoughts that when the man in black suddenly turned to face me to ask if I was enjoying the music, I jumped out of my skin, making him laugh out loud. Even more perfect! A film star, I presumed, unless he was a visiting Adonis from another planet. In my whole life I'd never encountered such an incredibly handsome and mysterious specimen of maleness. When my heart palpitations eased and my intense all-body blush abated, I managed a shy smile and an affirmative nod, after which we began to talk normally, or at least he did. I was being asked real questions about myself and my life, and never once did he turn his eyes away from my face or interrupt me, and he always waited until I had finished speaking before he responded. He seemed to sense my struggle to open up and encouraged me to say more by asking more. Conrad, my mysterious man in black, not only properly listened to me but also heard me, and that was all that was needed to open my heart and awaken my inner *me*, my true *me*. I could feel it preparing to make a grand entrance, and I wasn't afraid at all. The waiting was over, that special someone had come along to show me that I mattered. Needless to say, this was a pivotal point in my life that I was happy to accredit destiny with, because it brought two strangers together to seal a long and lasting friendship. I even took a year sabbatical from my job in London to go off to Greece with Conrad to run a flotilla. I knew nothing about sailing or about being a stewardess on board a yacht, but Conrad's confidence in my abilities convinced me to take the plunge and sail off into the sunset. Everyday I discovered new things about myself that I liked, and this filled me with the outer confidence that I had longed for. Was I blessed with this experience or what? So many happy and joyful memories to cherish.

So why am I finding the temptation to escape into my shell more and more appealing now? If I've learned anything in these past years, it's that "switching off" from what's in front of me is only temporary, because another scenario from another person with a different story but with the same reflexes and reactions is sitting in the sidelines waiting to jump in and offload their stuff. That's why my resolution must be a tool to help me stay focused and to deal with any awkward situations, without having to drop half my friendships. Using the right words must be important in my New Year's resolution as each will play an important part in its success. Whilst I recognise there is no power behind words like "perhaps" or "could" or "should" or "ought" because using them will only ensure that nothing gets done, ever, I'm still not convinced about what words I need to include. Affirmations are meant to inspire, motivate, encourage, and be a support for the changes that need to happen, which in my case will be to stay in the present, always speak my truth, and stop providing the kind of false support that keep my friends coming back for more. I find that after each interaction my energy is so drained that I have to rush to the nearest patisserie or junk food shop and load myself up with comfort food which wrecks my diet. It's time for me to win, or least deal effectively with the real issue that troubles me. This people-pleasing has to stop. Somewhere inside I know I have integrity and self-worth, and that's what I want to demonstrate. I must put myself first, and if that means I lose friendships along the way, then so be it. Others will come, because change attracts change, so they say.

This reminds me of when my dearest friend Jean and I were persuaded by her eldest son to enrol on a five-day personal awareness training that he said had changed his life. *"Never too late to be blown away,"* he said. I can't recall what I was so scared of exactly except finding myself, but from what I heard, I knew if I was to cease hiding my feelings and "switching off" for good, I had to do something radical. I discovered what that meant after experiencing the very first process on the very first afternoon. This initial process involved mingling with the twenty-five attendees and standing before each one in turn, while maintaining eye contact with them, and saying one of three statements that were allowed: either "I trust you," or "I don't trust you," or "I don't know whether I trust you or not." An opportunity to obey the rules exactly, but nonetheless terrifying. I didn't know which was worse; deciding what to say to the person or waiting to hear what the other person had decided to say to me. The temptation to take the coward's way out and trust everyone was huge, but somehow it didn't seem appropriate because everyone appeared as nervous as I was. By the end I was exhausted and grateful to be asked to sit on the floor, close my eyes, and reflect on the experience, and when the music started with Neil Diamond singing "Honesty," I totally understood what the process had been about. The lyrics were spot on and made me realise the importance of being honest and true in every interaction and how I avoided it. I feared the worst and experienced the best, which was a profound release, and a definite life changer.

As of this moment I intend to create an affirmation for myself to take into 2017 and beyond, in order that on January 1st 2017, my early morning meditation will for the rest of eternity be preceded by something along the lines of: *I Love and Approve of Myself, Open My Heart, and Listen with Love.*

Now I'm ready to welcome the New Year and in the meantime, I'll enjoy each day of Christmas movies and the hope that comes with them.

ODD ONE OUT
By Bethan Evans

6:28 a.m. on an early September morning.

The subtle chorus of bird calls was harshly split by a piercing bicycle bell as the advancing fingers of mist loomed over houses, inserting nightmares into the innocent minds of children. Gradually, the fog poured into Ember's bedroom, coating the walls with a hazy pattern contrasting vividly with the gentle illumination of dawn. It cast dense shadows onto the pale floorboards and smothered the figure that sat as if set in stone on the window ledge in a grey mass, giving the illusion that if she moved, she would merely be taken away with the wind. Every ounce of colour had retreated into the corner, and she stumbled, trembling, as the mist waited, as if it was teasing, and then—

BEEP! BEEP! BEEP! BEEP!

The fog poured out of the window while a yawning fourteen-year-old slipped, lost her grip on the dream, and began her descent to the floor.

Now that evil has been defeated, introductions may begin:

Ember is a kind-natured teenager who is currently attending a Boys Academy because it's the highest-achieving school in southern England, and even though Ember is a girl, her education-obsessed parents insisted that she was accepted due to her "exceptional skill to know everything."

111

Unfortunately, Ember seems to have misplaced this skill.

"Emmie, hun! It's your first day at your new school!"

"Mum, for the last time, please just call me Ember. I sound like a four-year-old."

"Okay then, Ember," her father replied in his harsh, mocking tone. "Why don't you use your intelligent age to get your tired eyes down here for breakfast!"

"Alright then, mardy."

Ember slid down the banister into her modern kitchen and came face-to-face with her father who didn't look so pleased.

It's essential you understand that Ember, her mother, and her father are the three most contrasting people you would ever meet. Valerie, mother, is essentially glued to the idea that her daughter is still her young baby. But Lawrence, father, speaks to Ember with such bitterness in his voice that you expect daggers to come soaring out of his mouth. He wanted a son, and now he believes that Ember will never amount to anything other than rehearsing scripts that he wrote to get her a glamorous, no-thought-necessary life. Ember's description of herself is rather shorter. She is a teenager who never fits in.

Fast forward beyond breakfast, her uniform, and minor disagreements, and the final destination is the dreaded school gates. Step-by-step Ember edged forward into the hollow building.Ornate structures clung to the walls like their last hope was painted there. A banner with the Latin emblem emblazoned across it was magnificently slung between the windows, shredding the light. Yet the only thought that occurred to Ember was why the school motto was in Latin. *Am I still in the twentieth century?* Unfortunately, her pondering was short-lived as when she turned to exit, Ember collided with another student.

"Hey, you must be Emily. I'm Eddie. First girl here, I see."

Still unable to talk, Ember managed a quiet, "It's Ember, actually, and do you know where I'm meant to be?" She cringed at how much she had sounded like a stereotypical schoolgirl.

"Well yeah, I'm collecting you to make sure you're not late. You'll get expelled otherwise."

"That wasn't really on my to-do list, so lead the way." Ember relaxed slightly. *After all, joking is what you do with friends...I think.*

"Ha! I'm rolling on the floor laughing. Come on, it's Philosophy now, and you really will be laughing if you get the teacher to like you."

There. It had begun.

Ember had to skip a step every so often to keep up with her guide and used the opportunity to observe the boy who could end up being her only friend. Eddie. Darkened by the shadows, his red hair had flecks of brown on the tips, his tie was lopsided, and his satchel was tarnished with specks of paint. His eyes were a murky blue, and whenever he looked at her, whether a glance or a gaze, Ember could see that he, like her, didn't belong.

Ember's day was word-for-word just how she had imagined it. Every lesson was miles away from the distance her brain could grasp, and nobody took the opportunity to talk to her, and if they did it was only to exchange insults. Eddie attracted a few people but only to gossip about Ember and the new breach of the school policy. Even though she couldn't evade the crowds, she'd never felt so alone.

Finally home, she opened the door and winced at the screeching noise it made as it caught on the wooden floorboards. She stepped inside her house. Everything felt unusual and out of the ordinary. Her father sat on the broken armchair in the front room. He smiled, but it didn't reach his eyes.

"Your mother has gone away. She's never coming back. She said that the stress was too much. Having a daughter was too much for her. She's gone."

Ember felt weak and held onto the door handle for support.

"No. She can't. She wouldn't. Even if she did leave, it'd be because of you not me." Her patience broke, and she yelled ferociously at her father. "Why didn't you stop her? I could've seen her one more time. Her, not you."

He rose from the armchair. "Are you saying I mean nothing to you? I am your father! Respecting me is your duty! I never loved you or your mother. You want to know why? DO YOU?"

Ember whispered her answer, filled with detest and disgust. "Because we're women. I'm sorry that you're not the king of the universe, and I'm sorry that me being alive as YOUR daughter is so painful for you! I CANNOT HELP MY GENDER, AND EVEN IF I COULD I WOULD NEVER DO ANYTHING TO CHANGE IT! You need help, not me, and certainly not my mum!"

Ember stormed out of her house with one destination in mind. The Boy's Academy. It was the only place she could be someone else, the only place where she had a chance left to change. Her father called after her, but she kept running. Ember's footsteps echoed across the long abandoned choir hall, and her tracks left fresh prints in the dust. Scouring in every direction, Ember's gaze eventually settled on the stage with the torn curtains and smashed window. Tears streamed down her face as she scrambled up the steps in the centre of the light. Her voice wavered, but Ember began to do what came most naturally to her. She began to sing.

Say be one of a kind
Say never change your mind
Say you are the only one fit for you
Say keep hoping got nothing to lose

And I keep repeating the rules of gold
And I keep saying the rules of gold
And I keep telling the rules of gold
Why am I doing what I've been told?

I'm not an angel!
And I'm never going to be

Because the perfect approach just isn't for me
I will be seen and heard
You may think for a girl that this is absurd

But I'm not an angel
And I'm never going to be
I'm not an angel
And I'm never going to be

Ember tried so hard to continue, but the images of her
mother, her father, the sounds of every insult, every word,
every voice that ever doubted her, screamed for her to stop.
Screaming that her stupid, good-for-nothing song was never
doing anything even mildly decent for her. Still, to prove
them wrong, Ember kept singing. The lyrics had never come
so naturally to her, the hate and the pain resounding in
every syllable she sang. Choking with sobs between words,
she grabbed on tight to the broken, old microphone, fearing
that if she loosened her grip, she would be taken away with
the wind.

"Why?" Ember asked. "Why do I have such a dark life with no light to shield me from the pain? If I'm left in the darkness, I won't be able to see the difference between it and myself."

Everything was so muddled and even worse, she had no one to help her. "What I wouldn't give for a light just now!" she pleaded, in hope that someone, somewhere, may listen to her.

It was then that she realised the truth of her name. She was a fire, and her embers were never burning out.

THE ROPE SWING
By Karen Waldram

You can't see it at first, especially looking down the valley towards the stream. But it's there. So thick that you would define it by its girth. Not by its ply or its gauge, but by its girth. I dwell on that. Girth: an old word of size and substance. A giving word, a telling word, a woman's word. It keeps things in their place. In insult or praise, the same— solid and dependable. In combination with the tree the rope becomes utterly solid and dependable. And something with that girth would be. Its girth is such that I cannot take it in my one hand.

I concede wearily to myself that my hands are small.

I walk downhill towards it, nearing a log long since fallen. The log will bear my weight. Seated here and facing directly towards the tree, I watch. In the middle of the wide open space; the tree. In the middle of the tree's barely open canopy, the rope. And there, failing to achieve symmetry, low below the middle of the utterly dependable rope, the knot. In need of something to look at, something to carry my thoughts away, yet not to bring them back, I watch the rope.

The rope hangs top to bottom, shadowing the length of the tree's deeply ridged trunk. Its source is hidden somewhere, maybe where the green opens itself to the blue. As gravity demands, the rope shadows the tree's height towards earth, so nature demands that the tree's life giving sap reverses the route of fall and rise. Forces to be reckoned with! The rope seems to have connected itself to the tree's life force, feeding on xylem, having not aged or worn in the years I have watched. Yet we both seem old today.

The knot holds its own dead weight near the bottom. I think of hands twisting the fibrous girth of the rope into such a knot. The thoughts which follow twist my mouth and gut. I force them down.

The knot is tied in the filthiest of ways. The deliberate outcome of a predetermined act. This knot being of itself remorseless and irreversible, its purposeful form intended to never give up its hold. Its image claws deep welts in the essence of my being. I scrutinise it. It holds my gaze.

Despite exhaustion I need my eyes open. Closed, they see too much. I choose not to take sharp focus, letting my memory be placated by the sideways gesture of the knot moving within and beyond my vision.

To and fro. To and fro.

To, the noose and fro, the knot.

To, your face and fro, the knot.

The knot blurs, and in my chaotic imagination, gargoyles spout vitriolic water at me, tiny vipers weave and thread inseparable bodies within the nest in my mind, and my severed head rolls away from the block. The mist rolls in.

The log will bear my weight.

I shift my steady gaze back to the tree. With Escherian trickery, the movement returns—right to left. The sway of the rope expands the tree's silhouette and grants it motion. The tree itself now expanded, now quickened, responds. It inhales, it exhales. It waxes, it wanes. It ebbs, it flows. It breathes, draws air in slowly. It exhales, slowly, leaving apologetic, depleted lungs. I watch the tree breathe. Breath feeds the heart. I watch the tree's breast rise and fall, and I feel each heart-pumping inhalation. As it breathes, so could it feel, and as it feels, so could it weep. I want the tree to weep.

The wind that has so far been a whisper becomes loud. Breathy and uncomfortable. Its discomfort grows. I listen as the wind becomes angry. I want to hear its voice, raised to a howl of pain. To hear the howl of injured human-animal pain. I want the wind to howl.

The howling voice of the wind scatters the lazy grains of dust around their parental stones. There is nowhere to hide. The stones are unmoved, impassive. My face, watching, is a stone. I want the stones to scream. I want the fucking stones to scream in a me-like voice with a me-like face. I want the stones to scream. The swing sways, and the girth of the rope pulls my eyes to focus. It hangs, straight. There is no noose. Although I wish there were. No noose, no noise. No more, no less, no you. There it is. The unbearable truth, hanging in silence.

He was not hung but stabbed. It was not this place, and it was not this day. But this place can bear things. The tree, the wind, the moor, the stones, they can bear such things. Even on this day when I cannot.

On this day that I cannot fight, I wedge my small fists into my soft flesh while listening for the howl, for the sound of a silent, stone faced scream.

In time, I draw out my fists from their prison-home between my thighs and wrap my empty arms around myself. I unclench from fists the hands which were large enough, once, to enclose yours. I unwrap my arms from the gut that grew your bones.

I stand, just a few steps away from the tree. I walk, where you would have run.

I step out of my shoes, as we both often did. I feel the ground beneath me. I take hold of the rope, feel its girth, solid, dependable. With a familiar two handed grip, I pull the weight of my you-less self onto the waiting rope, and swing.

BUGALOO: A VERY RARE BREED
By Robyn Nyx

My English hasn't always been this good. I was once an under educated canine of indeterminate descent. For my grasp of the language of poets, I have to thank My Rubi. My Rubi was the woman with the 7-Up, and she is the rescuer of my Doggy self. When I was left to rot in the searing heat of the Fuerte Venturan desert, it is My Rubi who saw me and with a swift flick of her Swiss army knife, released me from a fate I do not even wish to contemplate.

My new life began on the 31st January 1998. I had spent three days and two nights alone, tied to some structure at the end of an unfinished road, with nothing to eat or drink, and it's possible I didn't have much time left on this Earth. In the distance, I could see two figures walking towards me. I began to get very excited. Had my mum's owner reconsidered his cruel decision to abandon me and returned, full of regret and laden with tripe sticks, to collect me? As the figures drew closer, I could see that wasn't the case. These were two females: one was tall, imposing, and rather round. The second was similarly tall, but much slighter, and athletic in build. The way they reacted to my wagging body told me that I was a welcome sight indeed. There was much human noise in a dialect to which I was not accustomed, followed by the revelation of this "7-Up." I was fooled, you see, into thinking it was the lovely nectar of the earth that is water. Clear and cool was what I expected as it was poured into the hand of the slighter woman who was to become My Rubi. What I got was cold, but it had bubbles that seemed to explode in my mouth, and they tickled my tongue unlike anything I'd experienced before. Still, it could not be denied that it was a welcome and refreshing liquid that tasted all the better as parched as I was.

My Rubi took out a sharp implement, and with minimum effort, she released me. I garnered as much attention and love as I could, immediately sensing what was to become a lifelong, emotional, and inexorable connection to My Rubi. Perhaps I sensed that the other woman was not to feature in my life for the long haul, and for that reason, I wasted little of my very valuable devotion on her and focused my full and unadulterated consideration on My Rubi.

***

Our first day together was awesome but for one encounter. I was on the receiving end of the longest cuddles I could ever have imagined. My Rubi scooped me into her arms at every possible opportunity, enabling me to plant my very best kisses all over her face. Since I was not long in the world at this point, I have to admit that my breath was far more pleasant than it now is, and my kisses were something to behold. My Rubi revelled in them, enunciating poetic-sounding words that served only to encourage my affections.

It was at the beach, where I discovered I was not a fan of the big surf, that I had fleeting doubts that my new best friend had my best interests at heart. My Rubi tried valiantly to tempt me into the vast and foreboding moving water. Everybody knows that the wet stuff should be still until slurped. It should not surge towards an unsuspecting Dog in an aggressive and frankly, quite disturbing manner. Frothing at its peak like some sort of rabid animal, it wasn't my idea of fun at all. And yet, despite my quite obvious misgivings (I barked and ran to and from the sea, desperately trying to scare it away), My Rubi seemed determined to acquire my approval of the darn thing. Taking me in her arms again, My Rubi stupidly ventured into the ridiculously animated element and proceeded to disappear into it. The noise was horrendous. It was like the water was battering against My Rubi's body, and bizarrely, she didn't seem to mind one bit. Even as the water crept closer and closer to my tail, even as I dug my claws deeper and deeper into My Rubi's skin in an attempt to convey my dismay at being thrust into this dangerous environment, there seemed to be no end to the ordeal.

I began to wonder if this was a rite of passage into My Rubi's world, or perhaps a test to see if I was brave enough to become part of My Rubi's life. Briefly, I considered my position and wondered if I might have fared better tied to that pipe in the middle of nowhere. I think this might have been the exact moment My Rubi and I established our unique method of non-verbal communication, for almost as soon as I had contemplated that very thought, My Rubi beat a hasty retreat to the relative safety of the sandy beach. I'm a huge lover of a good sandy beach. Bullied as it is by the nasty and inconceivably angry sea, it manages to retain an aura of calm that encourages a sophisticated Dog like myself to dig into it and revel in its cool underbelly. Unsurprisingly ecstatic to be back on terra firma, I raced around the hot sand like a thing possessed, thankful to be unscathed by the whole episode and relieved that My Rubi was not some psychotic monster who took pleasure in the discomfort of the noble animal that it is the Dog.

***

My wonderful day was about to go drastically downhill. My Rubi was in what seemed to be a one-way conversation with a strange shaped piece of plastic that looked like it would be more suited as a plaything for me. It transpired that I was not allowed to stay in My Rubi's apartment overnight, and the resort management prepared a bed in much the same way as I had been used to:a blanket on the floor with my lead secured to a drainpipe lest I tried to escape. I found myself misunderstood. I had just found My Rubi. I knew we were to be companions for ever. Why ever would I run away now?

Nonetheless, My Rubi was obliged to follow the rules, and I shared the gut wrenching emotion My Rubi felt when she left me alone in the bowels of the reception building. I settled down to count the hours until My Rubi returned to take me for another day of exciting adventures.

***

When morning arrived, the "pool guy" released me and took me for a much-needed walk, although he did not use my lead and chose instead to call me to follow him. Fool. I followed him around for a little while but was soon tired of both him and his repetitive job. I was missing My Rubi and wondered when she'd return to rescue me from this monotony.

It was then that there was much "oohing" and "aahing" from the ladies carrying buckets, mops, and other assorted equipment I now associate with cleaning. Strangely, I was encouraged to follow them. I found this to be an interesting contradiction: I was being allowed to roam the resort freely when previously they had told My Rubi that I was not to be given free reign but questioning their human logic was, on this occasion, not for me. I was however, beginning to get a little frantic in search of My Rubi. I couldn't get a handle on My Rubi's smell at all. Her trail was eluding me, so I headed off the small resort in an attempt to find a stronger scent.

Have you ever been taken anywhere against your will? It happens to us Dogs all the time: especially to the white coated sadists who stick very sharp things into our skin and blunt things in places a human has no business being around. I suppose I wasn't actually taken without my consent. At first, I thought they'd be able to help me find My Rubi. The small human was on wheels, and this seemed to me to be an excellent way to cover far more ground in search of My Rubi. So when his mother scooped my little self up and dumped me in his lap, I can't truthfully say that I struggled. Their dialect was harsh and punchy, and it was yet more words that I could not understand. Nor could I make them it clear to them that I needed their help. When it finally dawned on me that they had no intention of helping me find My Rubi, I tried to wriggle free but the man-child would not let me go. He held on tight to my chain collar and just kept repeating the same thing over and over: "Hinsetzen, hund, hinsetzen." It seemed I was helpless again and that I would have to bide my time until I was heroically rescued by My Rubi. I was sure she would come. I had to be sure she would come.

∗∗∗

The way My Rubi tells it is like this: that morning, she and

Marian went to see how I was doing before they went for breakfast—someone told them the pool guy had taken me for a walk. After they had eaten, they tracked down the pool guy only to be told that the maids now had me. This angered My Rubi in the same way it had baffled me, but they set about looking for the maids with My Rubi beginning to worry about my safety. The maids added further fuel to the fire when they nonchalantly said that I had been running up and down, providing them with much merriment, dashing in and out of the apartments.

My Rubi was now loudly furious and stomped to the reception to demand two mountain bikes in order to widen and quicken her search for me. My Rubi covered much ground in her hunt for me, but it seemed I had disappeared from the island completely. Undeterred, My Rubi returned to her apartment and quickly created several posters in Spanish declaring: *PERDIDO PERRO—RECOMPENSA €50* which, for my non-Spanish readers means, Lost Dog— Reward €50. I'm aware that you might judge My Rubi for this seemingly low reward offer. Fifty Euros might not seem a lot for the return of My Rubi's new, one and only ever- to-be soul Dog, but you should be aware that My Rubi was not in particularly profitable employment at the time. In fact, she'd only just successfully secured her first post- University position two weeks prior to this holiday which she was clearly fated to take so that she could rescue me. In short, money was tight and €50 was all My Rubi had at this point, and she could only hope it would be enough to tempt someone into returning me to her waiting arms.

Posters in hand, My Rubi cycled all over the resort, taping them to all manner of lamp posts, sign posts, and fencing. Another circuit of the area bore no further clue as to my whereabouts. Returning to her apartment to create yet more Lost Dog posters, My Rubi was beginning to think that she had lost me forever, but she had no intention of giving up. Determined that we were to be reunited, My Rubi was about to set out for me again when the telephone rang.

I was in the possession of a German family, and they had come to claim the reward!

Learned as I now am with a thorough knowledge of the English language, I'm not sure I'm able to express how I felt when I set eyes upon My Rubi again. In the steely grip of the man-child on wheels, I'd wondered if the all too short a time spent with My Rubi was but a pearl in a vast mass of gritty sand that was to be my life. But when My Rubi pressed the Euro notes into the grubby little hand of the German boy and quickly scooped me up into her arms, I can only say that I felt this was where I belonged. Us Dogs are meant to be with you Humans and conversely, you need us too. I firmly believe that although our extreme good-nature means we can co-exist with almost any Human (however strange and weird—and you have to admit, you can be very strange and exceptionally weird), there is but one Human for each Dog and unfortunately, for the most part, the twain shall never meet. I had met my Human though, and I was not about to let her go again.

On Beauty and Tempering
By Marija Smits

Normal. What do you think of when you read or hear the word *"normal?"* I see a somewhat dull word for a rather strange concept, because if you think about it, nature never particularly aims for "normal." It specialises in diversity: big, small, fast, slow, loud, quiet, colourful, muted, and all that there ever could be in between. Yet *normal* is something that many, many girls and women want to be. For to be different—not *normal*—is something to be fearful of.

My parents had come to Britain from eastern Europe and so, although I was born here, I grew up understanding that I wasn't quite *normal*. Because *normal* meant you didn't have a foreign name. *Normal* meant you didn't eat continental food on Sundays when everyone else was busy tucking into their roast dinners. *Normal* meant you celebrated Christmas on Christmas Day not Christmas Eve. *Normal* girls didn't have eyes with strange lids that made them look *other*. And *normal* girls weren't big-boned and stocky with wide shoulders to match. In short, *normal* girls were, well, everything I was not.

Some of the pre-teen and teenaged boys I knew were also keen to point out what normal did and didn't look like. They were probably just as confused by society and hormones as myself and my girlfriends, but still...their taunts and criticisms stung.

Yet who was it, exactly, who gave me the idea of what was, and wasn't, *normal*? It took me a while to figure this out, but eventually I got there. You see, when I was about five or six I saw an advert on TV for a chewy peppermint. The rectangular mint was white with green stripes, and when the happy buyer of the mint, who happened to be clad in all-white clothes, ate the mint, green stripes appeared all over their whiter-than-white jumper. This was a mint I simply had to have. I don't recall how I got hold of one of those mints—I assume I must have nagged my mum into buying me some—but I still remember the disappointment I experienced when I ate the sweet and absolutely nothing happened to my clothes. There were no green stripes across my jumper, and the sickeningly sweet peppermint did not make up for this lack. Still, it was a useful lesson. I learnt that adverts are more fiction than fact; the products they're selling embellished with fantasy. In short, marketers lie.

But magically-appearing green stripes aside, what were the other, more pernicious adverts saying to us young girls? Well, that pretty was thin. Pretty was big hair, make-up, and the right kind of clothes. And this, the confusing dichotomy: pretty girls were sexually available yet also not. And at the very heart of the advert, there was the dark, dark lie: Your worth is measured by your appearance.

Now, I can see the lie for what it is, but back then I didn't, and I'm aware that I spent my fair share of cash on beauty products, clothes, and miracle diet food to make me look like the kind of person I thought I wanted to be. Because society wouldn't ever value me for just being me, would it?

***

I would like to live in a world where everyone is aware of

the dark lie, and are simply valued for who they are, but you see, there's two issues to deal with here. One, there's very little money to be made out of women who are confident in themselves and their unaltered appearance, and two, there's the basic fact that us humans are hardwired to judge each other's appearance.

Now, theoretically, we should be able to do something about the former issue, and in many ways we are—the backlash to Protein World's "Are You Beach Body Ready" ads are a good example of progress on that front (although sadly the company still received a massive boost in sales during the backlash) but the latter is actually much more complex because, for all our developed brains, we are, fundamentally, simply animals. And in terms of species survival, it's actually useful to be able to quickly assess another human by their looks. A person's appearance can give us clues about whether the person could be an ally or an enemy, and in some extreme situations these snap judgements can literally save our lives, propelling us to fight or flight. Love or loathe. Also, a human's facial symmetry, skin, and hair are good barometers of health. A person's overall appearance gives us an indicator of whether they could potentially harm us with a disease or make for a good, or bad, potential mate. For always, always, our genes consider the future, take calculations about whether or not a mate would give us strong, healthy children. In a language we cannot as yet quite fathom, genes speak to genes in a conspiratorial and silent symphony.

***

When I was in my twenties, I had an encounter with someone "different," and although I didn't understand its importance then, this encounter was to take on a new and meaningful significance to me a decade later.

One evening I was returning to the house I shared with my university friends, and in the dimly lit hallway I encountered someone I hadn't met before. A young Caucasian woman with a large purple mark that covered about half of her face. I can still remember the jolt of fear that ran through me when I saw her. This was a moment of animal clarity, all social niceties washed away by fear. The mark on the stranger's face was startling, and the fact that I had no reference to it, no experience to draw on deeply unsettled me. *What's that on her face?*

Thankfully, good manners and reason came to my rescue, and I greeted her and learned that she was a friend of one of my housemates. Later, as we sat around the kitchen table, I silently scolded myself for my reaction. The friend of my friend simply had a birthmark on her face, a port-wine stain. I wondered at my reaction. And I also couldn't help wondering how she must have felt. Surely I had gawped, surely she had seen the fear on my face.

Was I right to scold myself? Perhaps. Perhaps not. We must allow ourselves our genuine feelings. Yet if we are to extend our knowledge and connect with those who are different to us and whom we are, in the main, biologically and societally conditioned to gravitate away from, it is important that we become aware of this conditioning. And we moderate and temper it. We do this by setting aside the filters of prejudice and the mechanics of biological programming. We become truly open and receptive. It's a difficult state to achieve, but a state that I believe we should all strive for.

***

When I became a mother something happened that made me remember the encounter I'd had with the young woman with the facial birthmark. Shortly after my daughter was born, a few red spots appeared on the bridge of her nose, close to her left eye. We assumed it was baby acne. Yet within a few weeks the red dots had grown in size and joined up. She now had a bright red lump, about the size of a walnut, between her eyes. My husband and I looked at each other and wondered "What's that on her face?" It turned out to be a strawberry haemangioma birthmark. Thankfully our GP and various specialists who kept a close eye on my daughter's birthmark were able to confirm that it wasn't going to affect her health or vision.

However, as the birthmark grew, I underwent a crash course in biological and societal conditioning, and its very real effect on human interaction.

Young children would poke the birthmark, attracted by its redness and squishiness. Older children and adults mostly showed concern. Yet in some people's eyes, curiosity was tainted with the fear of "other," of "different," and of "I don't understand." But thanks to the encounter I'd had with that young woman, someone else's daughter, all those years ago I could empathise with this reaction. But this was now my daughter. Empathy was joined by an anger that burned white-hot in my heart.

"What's that on her face?" was a frequent question. I put on my scientist's hat and saw myself in the role of educator. I became adept at explaining: "No, it wasn't an injury or a sore. It was just a birthmark, a collection of proliferating blood vessels under her skin," and "No, it didn't hurt her," and "Yes, it would probably go away with time."

Most strangers, family, and friends were kind and said things that we understood as being well-meant: "Don't worry, I knew someone who had a birthmark and it disappeared by the time he was five," or "I had a birthmark too when I was little. It completely vanished though. I'm sure that'll be the case with your daughter." However, one elderly relative was utterly thoughtless: "I do hope it goes away soon. She'd be so beautiful without it."

And that is how we come, full circle, back to the dark, dark lie, be it uttered subconsciously or consciously. Your worth is measured by your appearance.

***

My daughter is utterly beautiful as she is, birthmark or no birthmark, because she is a wonderful person with a beautiful soul. I have watched her grow, mature, and cope with being very slightly different to the other girls in her class at school. In today's world, bombarded as we are with images of what we should look like and of the rightness of "normal" and the wrongness of being "different," it makes my heart swell with love when I hear my daughter say that, quite rightfully, she's okay about having a birthmark. It doesn't define her, but it's also a part of her, just like any other part of her body. And as much as I wish that she didn't have to contend with the issues that being slightly different present to her, that's not for me to decide. I would like to protect her from the world and its judgmental eyes as much as possible, yet it's not for me to deny her the opportunity of learning about perception, skewed as it can be by society and biology. If anything, it will allow her to open her own eyes to human foibles and give her the chance to temper her own spirit so that it becomes as strong and as splendent as steel.

WHO AM I?
By Pam Burrows

There's something about seeing your mum cry, whatever age you are, that makes everything seem all wrong. The strong, responsible gatekeeper who protects you from all the world's ills has gone off duty. Anything could happen. I was in my twenties when I saw my mum cry like never before. She became so child-like and so scared that I thought we both would break. She was trying to explain to me that she didn't know who she was, and that she felt like an alien dropped from the skies, neither connected nor, most importantly, belonging to anyone or anywhere. It sounds like a story of mental illness, and I suppose in some way it was. But it's really a story of emotional pain and a sequence of events that neither me nor my brother had a clue about.

My mum was born in Preston in Lancashire, and later my grandparents moved to Derby where she grew up. Only here she was, telling me through a flood of heart-wracking tears that she was born in Manchester. And those grandparents? They're not my grandparents. I'd unknowingly prompted Mum's sharing of her story by asking the simple question, "If you could have anything for Christmas, that money can't buy, what special thing could I make happen for you?"

It was days before I managed to piece the whole story together from various fragments of information; her single, Irish mother dying of TB shortly after giving birth to her, and the people I thought were my grandparents arriving at a Catholic nursing home to adopt a curly blonde haired girl, only for my dark haired mum to raise her arms from her cot, eager to be chosen instead. When Mum got married, her adoptive parents gave her all the information they had. It amounted to her birth certificate and an adoption certificate. All she knew about her past was that her birth mum had given her the name Margaret, and she was Catholic. To this day, Mum really doesn't like anyone to shorten her name. Margaret is the name her mum gave her, and for a long time that was all she had.

In this moment though, as she was telling me the story, her tears were driven by fear. Fear that once I knew the truth, I wouldn't love her anymore. My mum had lived for over sixty years believing that being adopted was something shameful to hide away. She had also spent the last twenty years searching on and off for a blood relation of some kind, an anchor to the real world. Proof that she really was someone. She needed her people. I remember her saying that finding someone would be incredible, but that the one thing she wanted more than anything, the answer to my question of the perfect Christmas present was a photo of her mum. Proof of belonging, and a connection to her real past.

At this point she still daren't tell my brother and swore me to secrecy because of her fear of rejection. So we set off as a dynamic duo to reignite her search for family, an adventure that was both exciting and laborious in equal measure. In the olden days of the 1990's family records were all about microfiche. Miniscule text on rolls and rolls of plastic film viewed through a magnifying screen. Ad nauseam. No search engine, not even a way to search a particular word or name. Coincidentally, I was working in

Manchester at the time, and we set off to sit in the archives of the city where Mum had been born, apparently in a sewing machine shop, long since demolished. Every time we'd set off with so much energy and optimism. Each trip would end with us exhausted. So many dead ends and a whole bundle of "well perhaps..." stories that we made up, trying desperately to piece together some kind of coherent sequence of events with virtually no information other than Mum's birth certificate and a baptism notice.

Over the years we ebbed and flowed, every now and again having another burst of trying to find something, some one. Then Mum had a break through. She uncovered her mum's death certificate. The details showed Leeds as the place of death, a cemetery just out of the city. Dad drove her up, and she was lucky to find staff in the office and a big, handwritten book, detailing all the names and dates of everyone in the graveyard. Mum gave her mum's name and date of death and waited. Then came the news.

"Yes, that's her."

Mum fell against the wall, repeating, "I can't believe she's here. I can't believe she's here."

But there it was, her name written into the book in 1938. A short walk from the office, and she was at the grave of her real mum. And a dozen other adults and children. The tuberculosis epidemic was so severe that people were buried several to a grave, but there, listed on the leaning headstone, was her Mum's name, Bertha Kelly, who died of TB at age twenty-six.

Now in her sixties, after surviving two bouts of cancer, my mum had found her mum and a place to come to for at least some kind of connection. If there's one thing true about my mum, she doesn't mess about once she's got the bit between her teeth, and she was quick to ask the cemetery about the actual place of death.

Her mum died in a specialist hospital for people with TB, right next door to the graveyard. She went straight around, and though it was by this time closed to patients, a fabulous caretaker—one of a few members of staff tasked with winding down the whole building—allowed them inside, and they soon found themselves standing in the ward where my grandma would have stayed. It was an art deco, wide, curved room with an entire wall of windows that looked out onto a balcony overlooking a beautiful tree-filled garden, and though it was autumn, and there were no blooms in sight, there was a long bed of roses right under the balcony. The hospital would have been quite new then and a world away from the Victorian design of most institutions at the time. The fresh air from the balcony, the breeze in the trees, and the scent of the roses wafting up would have been beautiful. It was a huge moment for Mum, knowing she was standing in a room her mum had actually been in too. Later, in the archives in Leeds, we found a photograph of the opening of the hospital with a row of dignitaries proudly standing next to a flourishing bed of beautiful roses.

I remember sharing the news with friends at the time, so pleased that there was some progress, at least something to help Mum feel like a real person. Little did we know then, this was not the end of the story.

A few years went by, and every now and then we'd pop up to the cemetery to plant flowers and clear the weeds. I painted the engraving of my grandma's name so it stood out in the long list. It seems strange even now to write "my grandma." It was such a long time before I cottoned on to the fact this wasn't just Mum's search, but mine too.

We saw things change over time. In fact, it was less than a year after mum and dad stood in that TB ward, looking out at the trees, that both the hospital and the trees made way for a housing estate, and all the history was gone.

Enter the computer age, and the biggest single shift in anyone's search for family. Mum inherited my old PC when I upgraded and wasted no time getting the hang of the ancestry websites where you could post messages with the names of people you were looking for. And sites where you could search for birth, death, and marriage certificates and buy copies that arrived by post. This was a whole new world but whilst Mum got very proficient at searching, helping lots of friends to find their relatives, there was nothing but dead ends for her own search. She was invited to be guest of honour at a reunion party for a family who didn't even know they had missing siblings until Mum joined them all up. She became incredibly skilled at finding pretty much anyone, except her own flesh and blood.

Until one day she received a message from one of the ancestry sites. It was from a woman called Jenny in Canada, and she asked if Mum could possibly be their family's missing baby. It was a bolt from the blue and was the start of the most amazing connection we could ever have imagined.

Jenny's husband, John, wasn't hugely motivated to explore his family history, but Jenny had heard his mum, Susan, talk about a mystery baby back in the 1930's. The story went that Susan and her husband were going to adopt her sister's baby but her sister died before permission could be given, and the baby went for adoption elsewhere. Susan Kelly and her French-Canadian husband married and had a baby, John, Jenny's husband. They were from Leeds before they sailed to Canada, where they lived for the rest of their lives and had two more children, Sue and Yvette. Jenny had time on her hands and the question mark over this missing baby from her husband's family fascinated her. The surname

Kelly was the link, and it led to her finding Mum's post about Bertha Kelly on the internet.

It was Jenny's first day looking.

But Susan's story and the dates didn't add up. She'd said that the baby was two years old, but Mum was already adopted before she turned one. It was a nice theory, but it didn't stack up. Except...everything else did. It turned out she wasn't the wrong baby, it was the wrong story. And there on one of the few documents Mum had successfully researched, the baptism notice, was the clue; the name Susan Kelly. Susan was witness to the baptism of Bertha's baby in Manchester, shortly before Bertha died. We may never know whether there was another baby. Mum has certainly done some searching, but what we do know for sure is that Susan Kelly was her Auntie. She was there at her Baptism and that John, Sue, and Yvette are first cousins. First cousins and the first blood relatives, the first real connection and sense of belonging my mum had ever known.

Mum and Yvette started a beautiful cousin connection over their computers and recently both had their DNA tested. At the age of seventy-nine Mum got scientific proof of who she is.

But I'm getting ahead of myself. We owe such a huge debt to Jenny. Her research had not only found Mum, but she had already uncovered cousins from the original Kelly family in Ireland which meant we now had a whole host of family waiting to get to know the "missing baby."

Mum and I headed over to Ireland and not only did we meet relatives, but they insisted on us staying with them at the farmhouse where my grandma was born and lived until she went to England. Everyone welcomed Mum and I with open arms and tears filled my eyes when we walked into the farmhouse for the first time to be greeted by champagne and strawberries and the words "Welcome home." Never was there a more important use for that phrase. Mum now truly felt a sense of belonging, knew who she was, a Kelly, and to top it off, she had a place to call home.

The Kellys showed us photographs, graves, places, and people. They threw parties and treated us like royal guests. We photographed everything! And then someone handed us a brochure celebrating a hundred years of the local school. And there in the pages, a picture taken of the pupils, the whole of the village school, infant and juniors, amounting to thirty children at most. The picture taken at the very time my grandma would have been attending that school. It only took a moment. We spotted her straight away. She looks like me.

Family? Tick.

Photo of her Mum? Tick.

Could it get any better? Just a little bit.

Our Canadian cousins decided to take a trip. Ireland first and then England, and they'd be staying with us for ten days. I thought Mum would burst with the waiting. It was everything she might have wished for and more. John, Sue, and Yvette were funny, loving, and kind. They made Mum feel totally part of the family. I've never seen her so happy. And when they left, I've never seen her so sad, like they took a piece of her heart with them.

The family connections continued, and now we know all about the folks who went off to America, including Mum's cousin Maureen. Maureen is Mum's age and a total travel bug. Her daughter let me know that they were planning a trip to the UK to visit her son who was studying at Oxford and asked if I'd like to surprise Mum by turning up in Oxford to meet them. Another first cousin to hug and share the Kelly smile with was too much to resist. I concocted a story about a work meeting in Oxford that was necessary but so short we could make a nice day of it. Finally, the day came and we set off by train. By now the secret was out, a slip on social media meant Mum knew there were going to be US relatives in Oxford, although for a sweet naïve moment she didn't realise it wasn't a coincidence. She said how glad she was to know in advance of choosing what to wear, she didn't want anyone to be ashamed of her. Note to reader, she always looks ready to meet the queen! It was a whirlwind, beautiful day connecting with people who already felt like family. And the physical resemblance was uncanny.

Fast forward to today, and we can only gaze back in wonder at Jenny's drive to find that baby. Jenny passed away this year and as her family grieve her passing, we also celebrate what a gift she brought all of us, the gift of a loving connection to real family. The DNA test also showed up a second cousin, one who didn't show up as related to our Canadian family. There's only one thing that could mean. It's the only clue in all the searching so far that might lead to the missing piece from mum's birth certificate; her father. Maybe there'll be a second story to write after this one.

And Mum's long held wish to one day have a photo of her mum had one last burst of magic from Maureen in America. Having lost all her stored family history in a basement flood a few years ago, she was shocked and confused one day to find something, right by the computer. A photograph taken outside the front of the farmhouse in Ireland, of my great-grandad and his favourite daughter, Bertha, before she went off on her adventures to England. Whoever could have guessed what that adventure would hold.

SURVIVOR
By Anusah VR

She was seventeen when he first laid his eyes on her. He watched her come home from college, help her mother keep Sahib's house tidy, write her assignments on the verandah of their makeshift-house, giggle with her friends, and go out in the evenings for some *chaat*. Occasionally, he would even board the same bus and follow her to her college. But not once, during the entire year that he obsessively followed her had spoken to her, save for the time he had asked to clean his car and another instance when he wanted her to buy hibiscus plants for the garden.

On the night of Diwali, with fireworks exploding into a million shimmering stars in the sky and delicate lamps lining the doorway of every house, he asked her to marry him.

The landlord's son wanted the servant's daughter's hand in marriage. He thought it was a story fit for a fairy tale.

She had declined. She wanted to study. She wanted to give a good life to her parents. She was far too young for marriage. Besides, he had spoken to her a mere two times before this proposal, she pointed out. She apologised after laying out her reasons. With a curt nod, he walked away. Five months later, she'd forgotten the incident. But he hadn't.

Carrying a bruised ego, he approached her. It was her face that had beguiled him. It was her face that would pay the price.

She was waiting to board the bus to college when it happened. She felt the ice cold liquid splash her face. A split second later her mind registered an acrid smell that surrounded her. That was when the unbearable pain started to melt her face. She could hear high pitched screams, only later to realise it was she who was screaming. She had never known pain and fear could be that strong.

Something inside her died that day. But she survived. Survival was the tragedy, she thought.

In a country where the justice system was riddled with loopholes and money trumps morality, she eventually became nothing more than a forgotten case file in a perpetually growing pile at the justice department. She didn't expect justice, not even for a second. Reporters came in flocks, some nondescript organisation gave attention to her plight, and as swiftly as they had arrived, they left. Once they had gotten their fill to cover the front pages of every leading tabloid and the organisation had accumulated enough goodwill by associating itself with the victim, she was forgotten.

She watched her parents run from pillar to post, pleading with the courts to open their eyes, to see the atrocious injustice of it all, begging friends and relatives for money for her treatment. Eventually, they too tired of her. Money began to dry up, and they were knee deep in debt after funding her tedious process of recovery. They didn't voice their thoughts, but she could see it in their lifeless eyes. She had become a burden. But they stood by her because of the unfortunate ties of blood. Friends trickled away. No one likes to look at a face this hideous, she thought. She didn't blame them, but the feeling of isolation asphyxiated her nonetheless.

Like any other young girl, she had carried dreams of growing up into an independent woman. Instead, she had been turned into something that was either shunned or pitied by the society she lived in. She didn't know which was worse.

Her views changed over the span of thirteen years. She'd always carry unmatched hatred for that man. Forgiveness was a fallacy. She wouldn't let him win knowing that he walked free. He hadn't even spent a month in prison. With a few rupees he had procured the bottle of acid. With a few rupees he had procured bail.

She wouldn't let society win. She didn't survive the horror of it all only to be at the mercy of others. So she rebuilt her life piece by piece. She realised she couldn't bank upon anyone but herself.

She started with baby steps. Looking into the mirror was a challenge in itself. She didn't recognise the shapeless mass of skin that was once her face. Months later, she reached out to a group comprised of souls who had survived the same horror she had. She finally found her support system. Isolation began to fade away along with the desperation she felt. She didn't have to fight alone anymore.

The world did not want to see the pain and heart ache that was used to glue the shards of her life back together. It's unpleasant. It likes to know that hope and perseverance won. It doesn't like the silent screams and uncontrollable crying in the dead of the night. It doesn't like the innumerable surgeries and scars left behind. It wants a polished happy ending. It is easy to cheer for a story of triumph. It is much harder to stand by a life crumbling to pieces.

It was due to this very reason that it didn't matter to her when the world applauded when she walked the ramp at an international show. The only thing that mattered to her was the simple fact that she hadn't let that fateful day dictate her life. What she had become was not because of it but in spite of it.

THE PORTAL DRAWS NEAR
By Nina Dauban

Time to be at peace with kin
Your own, each others, all therein
The love of what we do together
Why we're here, our mission forever.

The portal draws near, ours to make safe
Can we be trusted to open the gate
With gentle steps and warming heart
The truth of You with sensing arts

Let not your fears make lesser your try
For we know your devotion lives in the high
We feel your heartache, we hear your cry
We uphold your courage, your reason Why.

Creation asks for your hand, the great romance awaits
For we are betrothed beyond planetary gates
That you may feel her love, with every touch of another
Every look, every smile, every word that they utter.

Come dear beloveds, fill your hearts with the Vine
Let the fullness of love fill your every design
Step into the marriage and declare I DO
For destiny beckons, WE ARE WITH YOU.

With Special Thanks To:

The wonderful authors who submitted their stories

NIDAS

The Arts Council England

Supported by
**ARTS COUNCIL
ENGLAND**

global words

What's Your Story?

Global Wordsmiths is a community interest company which provides an all-encompassing service for all writers, ranging from basic proofreading to development editing, typesetting and eBook services.

Our education and cultural progamme offers a holistic range of services for all ages, including writing and photography workshops designed to suit the current curriculum, as well as a full range of publishing services from concept and design through to publication.

Our community focused work involves delivering writing projects to underserved and under-represented groups, giving voice to the voiceless and visibility to the unseen.

To learn more about our work, visit: www.globalwords.co.uk

Other books by Global Words Press:

Voices Through Time: Stories of the Workhouse
The Victorian Vale: Farmilo Primary School
Times Past: Young at Heart
In Different Shoes: Stories of Trans Lives
Patriotic Voices: Stories of Service
From Surviving to Thriving: Reclaiming Our Voices
Fractured Voices: Breaking the Silence
Don't Look Back, You're Not Going That Way
Peace by Piece
Speaking OUT: LGBTQ Youth Memoirs
Late OutBursts: LGBTQ Memoirs